A NICARAGUAN FAMILY

A NICARAGUAN FAMILY

By Michael R. Malone

Lerner Publications Company • Minneapolis

Website address: www.lernerbooks.com

A pronunciation guide can be found on page 62.

The interviews for this book were conducted in 1996 and in 1997.

LIBRARY OF CONGRESS CATALOGING-IN-PUBLICATION DATA

Malone, Michael R.
  A Nicaraguan family / by Michael R. Malone
    p. cm. — (Journey between two worlds)
  Includes index.
  Summary: Describes, against the backdrop of the history of the Nicaraguan people, one family's flight from Managua to a new life in Miami, Florida.
  ISBN 0-8225-3412-6 (lib. bdg. : alk. paper)
  1. Nicaraguan American families—Florida—Miami—Biography—Juvenile literature. 2. Refugees, Political—Florida—Miami—Biography—Juvenile literature. 3. Miami (Fla.)—Biography—Juvenile literature. [1. Nicaraguan Americans. 2. Refugees. 3. Nicaragua—History.] I. Title. II. Series.
  F319.M6M26 1998
  975.9'381004687285—DC21   97-13827

Manufactured in the United States of America
1 2 3 4 5 6 – SP – 03 02 01 00 99 98

AUTHOR'S NOTE

This book is dedicated first and foremost to the Roa family. From the moment of our first telephone conversation, Edgar Roa expressed an inspiring willingness to collaborate and a commitment to share his family's story that was motivated by a greater good—service to his community. I thank him and his family for their openness and honesty in trusting their truths with a stranger and am honored by our friendship, the fruit of many hours of meetings.

A special recognition is also due to Nora Britton Sándigo, executive director of Fraternidad Nicaragüense, and others in this Miami-based organization, which serves the Nicaraguan exile community. An indefatigable activist, Nora traveled from Miami to Washington, D.C., and from rally to protest to rally to persuade government officials to offer Nicaraguan exiles a chance to work and live legally in the United States.

While the Roas are fortunate to have attained legal status, tens of thousands of Nicaraguan exiles in the Miami community and elsewhere in the United States remain in precarious legal limbo. In a landmark decision in June 1997, a federal judge in Miami temporarily halted deportations of Nicaraguans and other Central Americans. His ruling encouraged the U.S. government to reconsider its immigration policy toward these people, who fled their country in search of freedom and relief in the United States.

I am indebted also to my editor, Domenica Di Piazza, whose precise questions and supportive guidance added immeasurably to the quality of this project. Finally, I thank my life partner and wife, Chris Kirchner, daughters, Raen, Kayla, and Trina, and my mother, Barbara Malone. Their support and understanding are forever appreciated.

A street vendor (above) *in León, Nicaragua, earns a living selling bananas. Murals* (facing page) *in the capital city of Managua depict the revolution of 1979, which toppled Anastasio Somoza Debayle and ended the nation's long-reigning dictatorship.*

SERIES INTRODUCTION

What they have left behind is sometimes a living nightmare of war and hunger that most Americans can hardly begin to imagine. As refugees set out to start a new life in another country, they are torn by many feelings. They may wish they didn't have to leave their homeland. They may fear giving up the only life they have ever known. Many may also feel excitement and hope as they struggle to build a better life in a new country.

People who move from one place to another are called migrants. Two types of migrants are immigrants and refugees. Immigrants choose to leave their homelands, usually to improve their standards of living. They may be leaving behind poverty, famine (hunger), or a failing economy. They may be pursuing a better job or reuniting with family members.

Refugees, on the other hand, often have no choice but to flee their homeland to protect their own personal safety. How could anyone be in so much danger?

Soldiers on patrol (left) pass through a village. Revolution and periods of armed conflict gripped Nicaragua from the early 1960s until the late 1980s, leaving many thousands of Nicaraguans dead, homeless, or orphaned.

The government of his or her country is either unable or unwilling to protect its citizens from persecution, or cruel treatment. In many cases, the government is actually the cause of the persecution. Government leaders or another group within the country may be persecuting anyone of a certain race, religion, or ethnic background. Or they may persecute those who belong to a particular social group or who hold political opinions that are not accepted by the government.

From the 1950s through the mid-1970s, the number of refugees worldwide held steady at between 1.5 and 2.5 million. The number began to rise sharply in 1976. By the mid-1990s, it approached 20 million. These figures do not include people who are fleeing disasters such as famine (estimated to be at least 10 million). Nor do they include those who are forced to leave their homes but stay within their own countries (about 27 million).

As this rise in refugees and other migrants continues, countries that have long welcomed newcomers are beginning to close their doors. Some U.S. citizens question whether the United States should accept refugees when it cannot even meet the needs of all its own people. On the other hand, experts point out that the number of refugees is small—less than 20 percent of all migrants worldwide—so refugees really don't have a very big impact on the nation. Still others suggest that the tide of refugees could be slowed through greater efforts to address the problems that force people to flee. There are no easy answers in this ongoing debate.

This book is one in a series called *Journey Between Two Worlds*, which looks at the lives of refugee families—their difficulties and triumphs. Each book describes the journey of a family from their homeland to the United States and how they adjust to a new life in America while still preserving traditions from their homeland. The series makes no attempt to join the debate about refugees. Instead, *Journey Between Two Worlds* hopes to give readers a better understanding of the daily struggles and joys of a refugee family.

Poverty affects many of Nicaragua's children (facing page). *Poor families sometimes dig through garbage dumps* (above) *to find food, clothing, and other daily necessities.*

Women and children pause in front of a mural honoring Augusto César Sandino, a Nicaraguan rebel hero of the 1920s and 1930s.

The engine buzzed on the silvery wing as the small plane drifted on a field of white clouds. From their seats, Fatima and Edgar Roa could see the Tipitapa River below. Off to the south, Ometepe Island rose green and lush out of the shimmering blue of Lake Nicaragua. The newly married couple had just left their home in Managua, the capital of Nicaragua, on their honeymoon. Fatima and Edgar were flying to Great Corn Island in the Caribbean Sea off the Central American country's eastern coast.

Fatima didn't know the woman sitting beside her, but the two began to chat. Nicaraguans are friendly and talkative. Even the war hadn't changed that. The Sandinista revolution, which had begun years earlier, triumphed in July 1979—a little over a year before the Roas' wedding. On the day the Sandinistas (a revolutionary movement named for Nicaraguan hero Augusto César Sandino) took power, most Nicaraguans—including Edgar and Fatima—celebrated the end of 45 years of brutal dictatorship by the ruling Somoza family. The

new Sandinista leaders promised to end years of injustice. They vowed to provide schooling and other opportunities for everyone, not just for wealthy people. Although Edgar didn't agree with all the Sandinistas' ideas, he and Fatima, like many Nicaraguans, were relieved that the bloodshed was finally over. They were excited for their future and for that of their country.

The United States had aided the Somozas for years, partly because the family allowed U.S. businesses to make huge profits in Nicaragua. Anastasio Somoza Debayle, who became president of Nicaragua in 1967, gained U.S. support because he was a tough anti-Communist. Somoza abused his power, however. He sent his opponents to prison or had them killed. Still, the U.S. government supported Somoza against the San-

Anastasio Somoza Debayle was president of Nicaragua from 1967 until 1979, when revolution in his country and mounting international pressure forced him to resign. He fled to Miami, Florida, and then to Paraguay, South America, where he was assassinated in 1980.

Many Nicaraguan families lack modern conveniences for doing daily chores such as washing clothes.

dinistas. The United States feared that if the revolutionaries won, they would set up a far-left or Communist government. But with most Nicaraguans in favor of overthrowing Somoza, the United States finally pressured the dictator to resign in 1979.

Somoza and his family left Nicaragua, as did many officers of the national police. But some supporters remained. The Sandinistas feared that with the help of the United States, these Somocistas (Somoza supporters) might attempt to overthrow the new government.

13

Nicaragua is in the tropics, a region that lies near the equator and that has hot and humid weather most of the year. Residents of Puerto Cabezas on Nicaragua's Caribbean coast head for the beach to cool off.

The Sandinistas were suspicious of anyone who was not on the side of the revolutionary government.

"*Dios mío* (my goodness), that's the Managua airport," Fatima said suddenly. Startled from a doze, Edgar peered down. Instead of the marine blue of the Caribbean Sea, the massive letters FSLN painted on a hilltop just outside Managua came into view. FSLN stood for Frente Sandinista de Liberación Nacional (Sandinista Front for National Liberation), the name of the Sandinista movement.

"Bad weather over the coast has required our return to Managua," crackled the pilot's voice over the plane's intercom system. Fatima and Edgar didn't have time to be disappointed. A tall, serious-looking man addressed the couple as soon as they stepped out of the plane. "You are Señor Edgar Roa and you, Señora Fatima Ayala? Come with me," he instructed. Edgar and Fatima glanced at one another, then followed the man as he strode toward the airport terminal. Other men followed behind them.

The officials led the Roas to an airport office. Inside, the couple faced a supervisor seated at a desk. Two women and several men—all grim-faced, solemn, and dressed in plain street clothes—fidgeted against the wall.

"What's happening? Why were we separated from the other passengers?" Edgar asked, as surprised as he

Drivers heading into Managua on the Pan-American Highway—Nicaragua's only major roadway—see the white letters FSLN on a hilltop near the city. FSLN stands for Frente Sandinista de Liberación Nacional, the name of the Sandinista revolutionary movement.

was angry. The supervisor glared at him. Suddenly Edgar realized who these people were. They were government police.

"Nothing's happening. Why were you traveling to the coast? What's the purpose of your trip?" the police supervisor demanded. The torn leather of the armchair crunched as he leaned forward.

"What are you accusing me of? What's the problem?" Edgar asked. "We're on our honeymoon."

"We ask the questions here. Just answer, nothing more," the man barked. "Take her with you," he said. Several police guards hustled Fatima into a separate room.

Through the thin walls, Fatima could hear her husband's voice. Then the Sandinista police began to question her. "Tell us about your husband's friends. What about Francisco Cuevas and Jorge Aguirre? And Fernando Gutiérrez?"

Fatima recognized some of the names. They were friends of her husband's. Others she'd never heard of.

"What were you doing last night at Las Mercedes Hotel? Why did you leave your car somewhere else?" the officer insisted.

"My husband and I had our church wedding yesterday. We stayed at the hotel for our first night together, then flew out this morning on our honeymoon," Fatima explained. Maybe this is all just a mistake, she

Edgar and Fatima (center) *make a toast at their wedding celebration in Managua.*

16

thought to herself. Maybe these police have confused us with someone else.

"Who was the woman you were talking with on the plane? Your contact?" One of the police dropped his briefcase on the desk with a thud and clicked the latches open. Slowly he removed a manila folder. "I have the answers," he said, his voice icy.

Fatima listened in amazement as he read from the folder. "Fatima Ayala, 22 years old. Daughter of Francisco Ayala, an office clerk, and Thelma Ayala. Nine brothers and sisters. Two sisters, Sandra and Marta, live in the United States. Fatima attended Instituto Cristóbal Colón High School. Husband, Edgar Roa, also 22. Youngest son of Adolfo and Berta Roa. Grandfather, Jesús Roa, made his fortune growing cotton and owns several *fincas* [big farms]. Edgar was a longtime member of the Boy Scouts. Honored by the Managua mayor for his idea to use plastic garbage bags in the capital. Attended the Instituto Nacional Central Ramírez Goyena High School. At 21, graduated in electrical engineering from Universidad Centroamericana, the private Catholic college. Employed for four months by Pennwalt, a U.S. chemical company." The officer stopped reading and looked hard at Fatima.

"Let's speak clearly, Señora Roa. The Revolución [revolution] does not accept traitors. Your husband is a spy for the CIA [U.S. Central Intelligence Agency].

Cowboys take a herd of cattle to market in western Nicaragua, where most of the nation's farms and ranches are located.

17

What is the secret message you and your husband were taking to the coast?"

"Nothing. We weren't taking a message," Fatima said. She had no idea the Sandinista government kept such detailed information about her life. She knew that Edgar opposed many of the ideas of the Sandinistas. But she was sure he was not a spy.

From the airport, the guards drove Fatima and Edgar to the Palo Alto prison. The police carried weapons under their shirts, and the Roas realized the danger of the situation. At Palo Alto, their pictures were taken. Afterward the Roas were forced to sit for hours and were forbidden to speak to one another.

Later in the day, the police released Fatima and Edgar. But first the couple had to sign a blank arrest form. They knew the police might later fill in the blank form to accuse them of a crime they hadn't committed. But Fatima and Edgar had no choice—either sign or stay in jail. The government police drove them back to Las Mercedes Hotel. The couple discovered that while they were being questioned, someone had rifled through their suitcases. Fatima and Edgar quickly gathered their things and went to get their car, which they had left with one of Edgar's friends. From there they drove to the nearby home of Edgar's parents. Edgar and Fatima didn't realize that their experience that day was just the beginning of their problems.

Fatima recalls the police interrogation she and Edgar experienced going to their honeymoon.

The largest republic in Central America, Nicaragua is bounded on the south by Costa Rica and on the north by Honduras. The Caribbean Sea, an arm of the Atlantic Ocean, stretches along the country's eastern coast. The waters of the Pacific Ocean glimmer off Nicaragua's western coast. About 4.6 million people live in Nicaragua. Nearly 70 percent are *mestizos*, people with mixed Spanish and Indian ancestry. Another 17 percent of the population have only European ancestors. Blacks (9 percent) and Indians (5 percent) make up the rest of Nicaragua's residents. Half of all Nicaraguans work in agriculture, the country's main industry. They raise beans and corn for the local population and grow coffee, cotton, and sugarcane to export (sell) to other nations.

In 1502 Christopher Columbus landed on the Caribbean coast of what would become Nicaragua. The explorer was fascinated with the tropical landscape, its natural resources, and the local peoples who hunted, farmed, and fished there. Columbus returned to Spain with parrots, gold trinkets, and other items

The ancestors of many black Nicaraguans were brought to the region as slaves during Spanish colonial rule. Other blacks fled to the region to try to escape slavery in nearby British colonies. Most black people live in poverty in Nicaragua's eastern coastal cities.

from the region. In 1524 the *conquistador* (conqueror) Francisco Hernández de Córdoba claimed the land and native peoples of Nicaragua as the property of Spain and founded the towns of Granada and León in western Nicaragua. For the next 300 years, Nicaragua was part of Spain's large colonial empire (overseas territory) and was governed by leaders in Guatemala to the north.

Many different groups of native peoples lived in Nicaragua. The Spaniards called the local peoples *indios* (Indians). Among the leading Indian tribes were the Niquirano, the Chorotegano, and the Chontal.

The Spaniards brought with them metal hatchets and shovels, seeds for crops, farm animals, and various handicrafts. In return for these goods, the Spaniards expected the indios to give sugar, bananas, rice, oranges, lemons, and tropical flowers as payment. Never before seen in Europe, these items were valued as treasures.

The Spaniards brought their religion—Roman Catholicism—to Nicaragua as well. They established missions, where they taught Catholic beliefs and Spanish culture to the native peoples. But the Europeans suppressed the traditions and customs of the indios of Nicaragua. The Spaniards also enslaved thousands of indios and shipped them to other Spanish colonies in the Americas to do hard labor there.

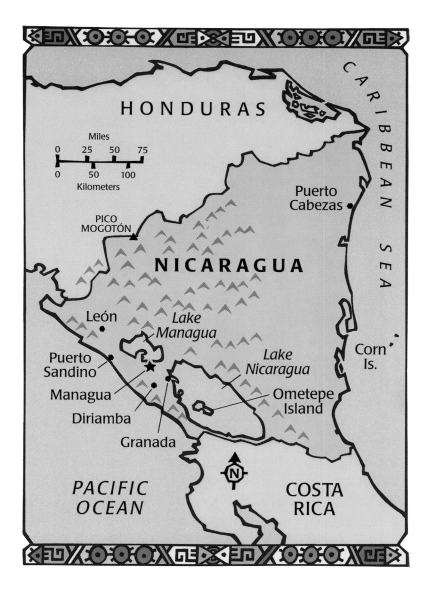

Central Nicaragua is mountainous. The country's highest peak is Pico Mogotón, which rises 6,913 feet above sea level on the border with neighboring Honduras.

CANAL POLITICS

The U.S.–owned Panama Canal to the south of Nicaragua dramatically reduced travel time between the Atlantic and the Pacific Oceans. To prevent other nations from building competing waterways, the United States forced Nicaragua to sign an agreement giving the United States exclusive rights to build a future canal across Nicaragua. In return Nicaragua received $3 million, but the United States demanded that Nicaragua use most of the money to pay back U.S. loans. The treaty was very unpopular in Nicaragua and throughout Central America.

In 1821 Nicaragua and its Central American neighbors joined the Mexican Empire and declared themselves free from Spanish rule. In 1823 the union with Mexico dissolved, and Nicaragua, Guatemala, Honduras, El Salvador, and Costa Rica formed their own joint federation. Nicaragua left the Central American federation in 1837, declaring its independence. Nicaragua's conservative, upper-class leaders were centered in the city of Granada. Liberal business-class leaders, on the other hand, were located mainly in León. During the early years of Nicaragua's independence, these two groups developed into the Liberal and the Conservative political parties. The two parties battled for power, and chaos and rebellion were common.

José Santos Zelaya, a Liberal, spearheaded a successful revolt in 1893 and ruled Nicaragua for the next 17 years. At first Nicaraguans supported Zelaya, who built schools and expanded railways. But Zelaya was a corrupt and brutal dictator known for his harsh treatment of opponents. Unpopular at home, Zelaya also made enemies in other countries. For example, he limited the right of the United States in building a proposed canal across Nicaragua that would link the Atlantic and the Pacific Oceans. With help from the United States, rebels drove Zelaya from office in 1909.

At about this time, U.S. banks began to lend money to Nicaragua, which did not have a strong economy

Crews began construction on the Panama Canal in 1906 and completed their work in 1914. The United States had originally wanted to build the canal across southern Nicaragua. But Nicaraguan leaders made demands the U.S. government didn't like. For this and other reasons, the United States decided to build the canal in Panama instead.

and which owed large amounts of money to the United States and to Britain. In exchange for the loans, Nicaragua gave control over its national bank and its railways to the U.S. banks. Many Nicaraguans were deeply unhappy with U.S. influence in their country. Clashes occurred between pro-U.S. Conservatives and anti-U.S. Liberals. In 1912, at the request of U.S banks and of Nicaragua's new Conservative president, the United States sent marines to keep order in Nicaragua and to put down the Liberal forces. The marines stayed to protect U.S. investments and interests in Nicaragua for most of the following 21 years.

In 1927 the U.S. government declared Augusto César Sandino an outlaw for his violent efforts to end U.S. intervention in Nicaragua.

Augusto César Sandino headed a rebel movement that opposed what he and many Nicaraguans viewed as interference in their country. Fighting from Nicaragua's mountains and jungles, Sandino and his supporters waged a guerrilla (nontraditional) war against the U.S. Marines. Despite their superior numbers, the U.S. forces could not defeat Sandino. When the marines finally withdrew in 1933, the United States turned over responsibility for maintaining stability in Nicaragua to the Guardia Nacional (National Guard). This police organization had been established several years earlier by the United States and was commanded by Anastasio Somoza García (Tacho Somoza).

By this time, Sandino had become a national hero. But because he opposed Somoza, the head of the Guardia Nacional had Sandino murdered in 1934. Two years later, in rigged elections, Somoza was elected president of Nicaragua and created a dynasty (ruling family) that held power for more than 40 years. During and after World War II (1939–1945), Nicaragua's economy improved by exporting cattle, cotton, and corn. Tacho—who owned much of Nicaragua's farmland—became the nation's wealthiest and most powerful man. In 1956 he was assassinated and his oldest son, Luis Somoza Debayle, became president. By 1967 Luis was dead of a heart attack. His younger brother, Anastasio Somoza Debayle (Tachito), assumed the presidency.

While Tachito was president of Nicaragua, the wealth and power of the Somoza family expanded greatly. The family owned and operated ranches, meat-packing plants, coffee and cotton plantations (farms), banks, hotels, newspapers, television stations, the national airline, and the country's only cement factory. Somoza and his family lived like kings, while most Nicaraguans remained desperately poor. Corruption among government officials was widespread. And anyone who opposed the Somoza government risked being harassed, imprisoned, or killed by the Somoza-controlled Guardia Nacional.

In 1972 a major earthquake devastated Managua. Many countries around the world sent money and supplies to help the thousands of Nicaraguans left homeless by the disaster. But Somoza kept much of the relief money for himself. He reaped huge profits by requiring that construction companies use cement from his factory to rebuild the city. And members of the Guardia Nacional sold some of the relief supplies for their own profit.

By this time, many Nicaraguans had become deeply dissatisfied with the Somozas, and some young

The earthquake that struck Managua in 1972 killed thousands of people and destroyed most of the city.

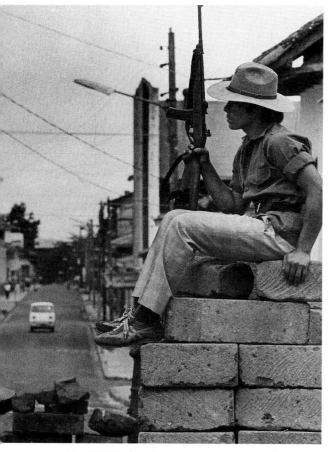

By 1979 the Sandinistas controlled most of Nicaragua's major cities. This Sandinista guards a barricade in Jinotepe in southwestern Nicaragua.

Nicaraguans had banded together to fight a guerrilla war against the regime. The rebels called themselves Sandinistas in honor of the national hero, Augusto César Sandino. Many Nicaraguans supported the group, known officially as the Frente Sandinista de Liberación Nacional (FSLN) in Spanish. The FSLN began to win battles in the countryside and then directed the war toward the capital in Managua.

In 1978 Pedro Joaquín Chamorro, a popular newspaper publisher and opponent of Somoza, was gunned down in the streets of the capital. His murder sparked a massive revolt against the Somoza dictatorship. Because of the strong opposition to Tachito, the United States pressured him to resign from power.

In early July 1979, about a year before Fatima and Edgar were married, the final FSLN offensive reached Managua. The rat-a-tat-tat of machine guns and the explosions of bombs sounded as FSLN soldiers clashed with Somoza's soldiers in the capital. Sharpshooters perched in trees and fired at anything that moved. On July 17, Somoza boarded a plane with his family, close friends, and political supporters and fled to Florida. Two days later, the last of Somoza's supporters surrendered. The war had devastated the country, leaving 40,000 dead in the fighting, 200,000 families homeless, and 40,000 children orphaned.

Fatima and Edgar met at a party when they were both 19. Young Nicaraguans love parties, and they don't need much to have one. Just some *marimba* music for dancing, Coca-Cola to drink, and the fun begins. Fatima and Edgar married at 22. Like most Nicaraguans, they had two weddings. First a civil marriage performed by a judge in November 1980 at the home of Fatima's parents. One month later, the couple had a larger church wedding for friends and extended family.

After the police detained the newlyweds at the Managua airport, they lived for about 18 months with Edgar's parents. A few months after the wedding, Esso Standard Oil—the largest oil company in Nicaragua at the time—offered Edgar a better position as plant engineer. He accepted happily and left his job at Pennwalt.

Soon Edgar and Fatima were able to move into their own home, a three-bedroom cement structure in a middle-class neighborhood. Except for the Roas and two other families, everyone in their neighborhood participated in the Comités de Defensa Sandinista (Sandinista Defense Committees, or CDS), neighborhood policing organizations. By joining the CDS, people received government-controlled supplies of food

Some of the buildings in this Nicaraguan town have graffiti related to the Sandinista revolution.

Edgar talks about life after the revolution in Nicaragua. At first the Sandinista government received money and support from countries around the world, including the United States. But the United States disliked Nicaragua accepting assistance from Communist nations, with whom the United States was not friendly. The United States also charged Nicaragua with supplying weapons to rebels in other Central American nations. For these reasons, the United States cut off aid to Nicaragua.

and gas. The committees encouraged support for the new government and its reading, health, housing, and sports programs. The committees also watched for neighborhood crime. Their policing efforts helped reduce violence, petty thefts, and other crimes. The committees were responsible, too, for reporting anti-government activity.

Edgar did not participate in the CDS. He got the gas he needed at Esso, and his good salary allowed him to buy food for his family on the black market. Through this illegal market, people could buy anything they

Karen was born in Managua in 1982.

wanted. You had to pay more, but you didn't have to wait in long lines for the inferior goods the government provided.

Edgar and Fatima avoided government programs such as the CDS. But this caused them trouble. The harassment began at night. Someone might pound on their door or toss pebbles at their windows. Graffiti, such as "Somocistas" or "CIA," were scrawled on their walls. Edgar and Fatima didn't support Somoza, and they were not spies for the CIA. Edgar remembers, "My family and my job were all that mattered to me. I just wanted to be left alone."

Fatima's sister Marta had gone to the United States many years earlier to study. Marta married a man in New York, became a hairdresser, and then moved to Miami. Marta wrote letters. "Come to the States, Sister. The Sandinistas are Communists, don't you see?" At first Fatima ignored her sister's pleas to leave. After all, this was her country, the only life she knew.

 Karen—the first of Edgar and Fatima's three children—was born on February 23, 1982, after a difficult labor. By the next year, antigovernment forces known as contras (short for "counterrevolutionaries") had begun attacking certain government operations in Nicaragua. Many of the contras were former Somocistas. They received weapons and money—secretly at first—from the United States.

In September 1983, contras dynamited a petroleum supply line at Puerto Sandino, a harbor on Nicaragua's Pacific coast. The Sandinistas accused Edgar, who had risen to supervisor of the Undersea Department at Esso, of supplying the company's engineering maps to the contras. He was interrogated repeatedly. Each day the police called him on the phone. "Is there anything you want to tell us?" they asked. Police also came to the Roas' home to question Edgar further. It seemed they would not leave him alone.

In October Fatima flew to Miami with baby Karen. Four months pregnant with the couple's second child, Fatima was to be the matron of honor at her sister Sandra's wedding. But Fatima had other things on her mind, too.

From her sister's house in Miami, she called Edgar daily and tried to convince him that they should leave Nicaragua. But he was hesitant. He held a prestigious job with an important company and earned a good salary. He had many friends, and his family was well respected. And in the United States? He would be just another worker, one of many looking for any job to survive. And besides, he didn't want to be a *gusano* (which means "worm"—an insulting name for Nicaraguans who had left their country).

When the Somozas were in power, they owned much of Nicaragua's farmland. After the revolution, the Sandinistas set up state-owned cooperative farms, where families would share in the profits of the land they worked. But with old equipment and low prices for crops, many farmers left the coops and moved into the cities. These young boys grew up on a cooperative in northwestern Nicaragua.

Sandinista forces battled the contras (above) throughout the 1980s. The contras received their money, supplies, and training from the United States, while the Soviet Union, Cuba, and many western European countries aided the Sandinistas.

But Fatima was afraid. Edgar was being harassed because he didn't support the Sandinista government. And the contras were winning battles in the north near the Honduran border. Bloodshed and conflict were increasing. Fatima felt she could not raise her children safely in Nicaragua. "We can make it here [in the United States]," she told Edgar. "You've got to leave Nicaragua."

Edgar had never imagined he would leave Nicaragua. But for his safety, his future, and for the benefit of his children, he made the most difficult decision of his life—to leave his homeland.

Edgar arrived in Miami on December 24, 1983. The family spent Christmas and Three Kings Day (Epiphany, a religious holiday in early January) at Sandra's house. When the holidays ended, Edgar went to the Immigration and Naturalization Service (INS) office in Miami. First things first. He needed a work permit and permission to remain legally in the United States.

Edgar filed for political asylum, a status granted to people who face danger or persecution in their homelands. In Nicaragua Edgar had been pressured and harassed—first at home and in his neighborhood, then at work. But this proof lay 700 miles away. In Miami Edgar had no papers and no witnesses. Edgar and others seeking asylum had heard of rude and sometimes

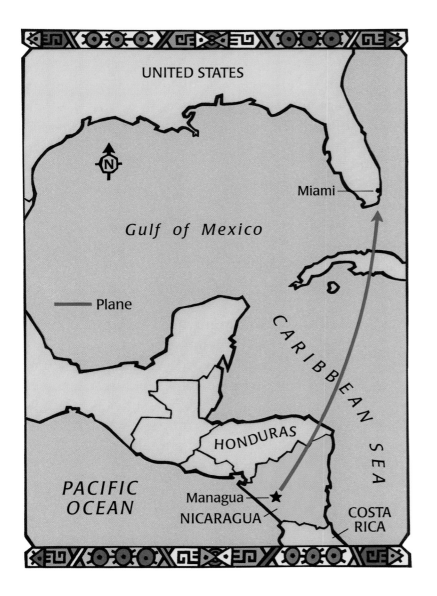

Miami lies about three hours by plane from Managua.

Students in Managua do their lessons in a school that was badly damaged by the 1972 earthquake. Rebuilding the capital continued into the 1990s, more than 20 years after the quake leveled the city.

hostile treatment in U.S. courts. Some judges seemed to feel that darker-skinned newcomers who spoke little English only wanted a free ticket into the United States. These judges had the power to decide whether to send immigrants back home or to let them stay.

The INS denied Edgar's first claim for political asylum. We have no documentation that you face danger if you return to Nicaragua, the INS wrote. All the same, Edgar received a legal work permit, which allowed him to stay in the country temporarily. Like many other Nicaraguans in the United States, Edgar and his family lived in legal limbo year after year, not knowing if the U.S. government would suddenly send them back.

When Edgar left Nicaragua, he had brought a job offer with him from an oil-refining company in Houston, Texas. But when he arrived in Houston, the company had given the job to someone else. Edgar sent out hundreds of résumés, hoping to land a job as an engineer somewhere else. When companies called back, however, Edgar had a hard time understanding them and making himself understood in English. In Nicaragua Edgar had studied English in school. When he came to the United States, he thought he could speak English. Yet reciting from a textbook and copying vocabulary words did not prepare Edgar for finding a job in an English-speaking country.

Two months went by. The money the family had saved was almost gone. Finally Edgar got a job as a laborer, building platforms for oil drilling in the Gulf of Mexico. The job was in Basile, Louisiana, so the family moved there.

Basile is a small town that lies two hours by bus from New Orleans. Main Street is the only road. No movie theater. One school. One gas station. One doctor. A health clinic and a few stores. The family rented one side of a double trailer from a Nicaraguan who owned the gas station and who had lived in Basile for more than eight years.

In the 1980s, when the Roas moved to Basile, black people and white people still used separate public rest rooms and separate entrances at the clinic. Townspeople viewed the Roas and the few other Hispanics in Basile as whites, despite their darker skin color. "One day after the end of a workday, I said to my boss, a black man, 'Come on, we want to invite you for a beer, it's your birthday,'" Edgar remembers.

"I can't," Edgar's boss told him. "Blacks here don't drink in the same bar with whites."

"That shocked me. We weren't used to that in Nicaragua," Edgar says.

Every day before the sun was up, Edgar bounced along in the pickup truck that took him to the Gulf coast. Most of the crew were black, but some of them

Workers drill for oil at giant offshore platforms in the Gulf of Mexico. Edgar's first job in the United States was building these platforms.

Eskarleth automatically became a U.S. citizen because she was born in the United States.

were Hispanic like Edgar. He earned $5.50 an hour, worked all day, and returned late in the afternoon covered with muck and seaweed from the Gulf.

Soon after moving to Basile, Fatima was ready to deliver her second child. But with no medical insurance and limited savings, she and Edgar worried about how they would pay for the doctors and the hospital. Since there was no hospital in Basile, the family traveled to Lake Charles, Louisiana, about two hours away.

Edgar brought his dictionary to the hospital because no one there spoke Spanish. He wanted to be prepared to talk with the doctors in case Fatima had problems, as she had when she gave birth to Karen in Nicaragua.

"Here, Doctor, *por favor* [please], this is a letter from Fatima's doctor in Nicaragua. It explains all about her condition and the complications from the first baby," Edgar said, thumbing through the dictionary to explain the medical terms. Though the doctor couldn't read Spanish, he delivered the baby and Fatima in good health.

Eskarleth Arianne Roa was born on April 13, 1984. Named after a Czechoslovakian doctor who was especially kind to Fatima in the hospital, Eskarleth attracted attention at the small hospital. She had creamy dark skin and a head full of coal-black hair that stood on end. The Roas followed the Nicaraguan custom of piercing their daughter's ears just after birth, and the nurses flocked to see the little girl with her twinkling earrings and little bracelets.

When leaving the hospital, the Roas got ready to pay their bill. "Don't worry," the clerk said. "This is a charity hospital. The state of Louisiana will pay your bill. But you can make a donation if you like."

The couple gave $300, as much as they could. They left the hospital and searched for a church. Religion for the Roas, as for most Nicaraguans, is an anchor in their lives. They found no Catholic church but stopped instead at a small, wooden, Baptist church. A few black worshipers prayed quietly inside. Edgar and Fatima entered with Karen and baby Eskarleth, kneeled, and said a prayer of thanks for the safe delivery of their daughter and for the generosity of the hospital.

This fresco (painting) adorns a wall in the main Catholic cathedral in Managua. The Roas, like 95 percent of Nicaraguans, are Roman Catholic.

In July 1984, the family moved back to Miami. "We wanted to improve our lives and thought that being closer to relatives and other Hispanics would help," they remember. Edgar, Fatima, Karen, and baby Eskarleth moved into a two-bedroom apartment with Sandra and Miguel, Fatima's sister and brother-in-law. Airplanes roared overhead day and night. Despite the brilliant Miami sunlight, the air always seemed hazy with exhaust fumes from the planes. Everywhere was cement and concrete. Still the neighborhood was nearly all Hispanic. In the shops and markets, everyone spoke Spanish. The Roas felt more at home in this place where people used their language and shared their customs.

Edgar, who had been an engineer in Nicaragua, took a job bagging groceries at a local grocery store. He worked briefly on a roofing crew, then took a job as a maintenance mechanic with a shoe manufacturer. For the next few years, he worked the graveyard shift, from 11 P.M. to 7 A.M., servicing and repairing shoemaking machines. In the evening, before going to work, he studied for several hours with other adults at a Miami high school to earn his electrician's license.

In the afternoons, Edgar tried to sleep for a few hours in the family's small apartment, but airplanes droned overhead, the phone rang, and the children chattered. To stay awake while he worked, Edgar drank *coladas*—strong, syrupy Cuban coffee laced with sugar.

Fatima found a job cleaning offices and businesses in the afternoons. So that Edgar might get a few hours of sleep, they hired a Nicaraguan *muchacha* (young girl) to watch the children while Fatima was at work. After Edgar earned his electrician's license, he got a job

A boy stands in front of a mural of Daniel Ortega (above), *who was elected president of Nicaragua in 1984, the same year Eskarleth* (left) *was born. Ortega served until 1990.*

with Peerless Electric and then with Aneco, one of the biggest companies in the Miami area. With Edgar's job situation improved, he and his family moved from the tiny apartment near the airport into a duplex in Hialeah, a mainly Hispanic city in the Miami area. The Roas' son, Edgar, Jr., was born in Hialeah in 1988.

Most of the Roas' neighbors were part of Miami's large Cuban population, including Lea Zipp, who owned the duplex and lived next door. Her cats, hundreds of them it seemed, roamed the property. The

Fatima and Edgar, Jr., share a laugh.

Roas kept to themselves. "We said *buenos días* [good day] and how are you. Nothing more than that," Fatima remembers. Immigrant neighborhoods are often transient—people come one day and are gone the next. With jobs hard to find and money scarce, constant change becomes a part of life. It's hard to establish roots and to feel part of a community.

Karen attended the nearby elementary school, and Eskarleth went to a day-care center. Fatima and Edgar always spoke Spanish with the children. But outside the home, the girls heard English. Watching the popular children's television show *Sesame Street* helped them a lot, too, and they learned quickly. Before entering school, the girls took an exam to test their English skills. Karen didn't need any extra classes. Eskarleth, on the other hand, was scheduled for classes in ESL (English as a Second Language) to help improve her English.

Before long Edgar's company promoted him to field supervisor. One day the company's president visited the construction site, and Edgar recognized an opportunity to make a good impression on his boss.

"You know, I can do more for the company than I'm doing now," he mentioned to the president as they toured the construction site.

"What? What can you do?" the boss asked, surprised by Edgar's assertiveness.

Edgar has worked hard to provide a good life for his family in Miami.

Edgar poses with Eskarleth and Karen (left) *in the backyard. Colorful toys* (below) *are among the family's favorite Nicaraguan crafts.*

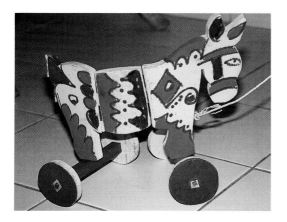

"In Nicaragua, after college, I worked as an estimator on construction projects," Edgar replied.

"Oh yeah? What was the biggest job you bid?"

"I bid on an entire hospital, one with 600 beds," Edgar answered.

The boss continued to quiz Edgar. Satisfied with his skills, he decided to reward this confident immigrant. Two weeks later, he promoted Edgar to the front office. First Edgar answered phones and company correspondence. "Talking every day on the phone and writing letters really helped my English to improve," he remembers. Used to estimating construction costs and materials the old-fashioned way, with pencil and paper, Edgar was unfamiliar with computers. But the company trained him, and he learned quickly.

"That was my big break. The company really treated me well. They appreciated my work and paid me well," Edgar says. But a slowdown in construction caused the company to lay off workers. Edgar was among the last to be let go in 1991. By that time, Edgar had his contractor's license and the training to start his own small company.

Within a few years, Edgar's own small construction company had earned a good reputation. Profits improved, and the family saved enough money to buy their own home. The house is located in Kendall (a Miami suburb) not far from Little Managua—a largely Nicaraguan neighborhood. The family's neighborhood sprawls with malls, glistening white condominiums, and swaying palms. Traffic is heavy just about any time of day, and construction workers hammer away even on the weekends. Sprinkled among the McDonald's and Home Depot stores are Latin *cafeterías*. These little restaurants, common throughout Latin America, sell Cuban coffee in tiny cups—little more than a thimbleful for a *café negro* (black coffee). Customers can also order beans and rice, *maduros* (sweet plantains), and *pasteles* (buttery pastries filled with cream cheese and tropical fruit).

The Roas' home is a two-storied, white stucco, Spanish-style home with an orange tile roof. Clown fish and guppies swim in a colorful fish tank in the living room. The sofa and chairs are made of rattan (palm wood), and most of the floors are tiled. Throughout the spotless home are paintings and other arts and crafts from Nicaragua. A brightly colored, wooden, toy horse reminds Fatima and Edgar of the playthings they knew as children.

Eskarleth is 12 years old. She shares her bedroom with her older sister, Karen, who is 14. Their 9-year-old brother, Edgar, Jr., has his own room. When they were younger, the two sisters used to argue, but things are different now. "She's like the biggest, best friend I've ever had. I tell her everything. If I tell my friends at school, they all gossip, but I trust my sister with everything," Eskarleth says.

Fatima keeps a close eye on the children. In the United States, she says, children have too many freedoms, and there is "too little respect for parents and grandparents."

The Roas are a close-knit family, and Fatima and her daughters enjoy many social and recreational activities together.

The Roas stay very involved in their children's lives. Instead of sending the girls off with their friends to watch a concert, for example, Edgar may take them. If the girls want to go to a movie with their friends on a Saturday afternoon, Fatima will go along.

With Edgar's good salary, Fatima no longer has to work outside the home. She devotes her time to the children. Every morning she drives them to school and meets them afterward. Recently Karen complained that her friends made fun of her for being driven to school, so Fatima agreed to let her take the bus. "But only if you keep your grades up," she warned.

Karen is one of 5,000 students at Braddock High School. Eskarleth attends seventh grade at nearby Hammocks Middle School. Like Braddock and Hammocks, most schools in Miami are large and overcrowded. Miami is one of the fastest-growing cities in the country, with many new immigrants arriving each year from all over the Americas. One day in Eskarleth's social studies class, the teacher asked whose parents had immigrated to the United States. Nearly all the students, including Eskarleth, raised their hands. Neither Eskarleth nor her sister Karen say they have experienced discrimination because of their heritage. But they know from their civics class that many people in the United States are disliked, ridiculed, and even harassed because of their ethnic and racial heritage.

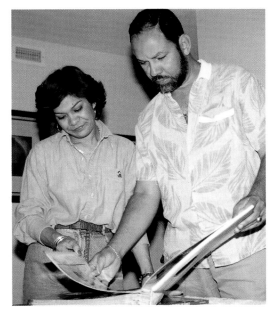

Edgar and Fatima look through the family's photo album.

The Roas gather on the couch for their weekly Bible-study session.

Eskarleth has school friends from Puerto Rico, Haiti, and Colombia. But most of her friends come from Nicaragua, or Nica, as Nicaraguans often call the country. "It's like a little Nica group, and we hang around together. We always talk about Nicaragua—like Nica this, or Nicaragua is number one. Even if some people like me who were born here, but their parents are Nicaraguan, we still talk about Nicaragua."

Eskarleth is a good student, and this year she made the honor roll. Technology class, where students learn on computers, was her favorite class last year. This year she likes drama and English. "Last year I wasn't so good in math, but this year I'm getting straight As," she says. "I'm really going to work hard because I want to start practicing for high school to get my grades really good. My mom told me if you get good grades, you can do anything you want," she adds.

In the Roa household, privileges are earned. No phone calls allowed during the school week. No sleeping over at girlfriends' houses.

"The children have their responsibilities, and if they want something, they have to earn it," Fatima says. "You want to go to your friend's house? Okay, then fold up your clothes. You want new socks? Okay, then clean up the house or take care of your brother while he's out riding his bike."

Last year, influenced by one of Karen's friends, Eskarleth became a raver. Ravers, she explains, dance to easy calypso or reggae music. They wear bell-bottom jeans, tops with wide, loose sleeves, and large, plastic jewelry—just like teenagers did in the 1960s. Fatima tolerates this new craze to a point.

"Well, the wide pants, okay, but not too much. She has to look like a girl. I don't want her looking like she's in a gang or something." Fatima says. She remembers that she chose her own clothes when she was a teenager, but her mother was always the final judge.

Eskarleth and her mother are close. Among their favorite things to do together is to go shopping. They often go to Rave, a clothing store at a nearby mall. There Fatima pays, but they both have to agree on which clothes to buy. Eskarleth saves her own money, too, for clothes and other things.

"Sometimes I save half my lunch money, but most of my money comes from selling Blow Pops," she says. Eskarleth buys a bag of the gum-filled candy for $2, then resells them to friends for a profit.

Every Thursday evening after dinner, the Roas unplug the telephone and turn off the television. They bring their Bibles and rosaries to the family room. Just as in Nicaragua, the Catholic religion is an extremely important part of the family's life in the United States.

Eskarleth poses in one of the outfits she wears when she goes dancing with her friends.

Eskarleth and Karen (above) *enjoy Nicaraguan dishes such as beef wrapped in banana leaves with boiled yucca* (below).

For an hour or more, they sit together on the blue leather sofa. They take turns reciting passages from the Bible and saying the prayers of the rosary in Spanish.

Sunday is family day for the Roas, and every Sunday begins with Mass at Good Shepherd Catholic Church. Because so many people in the community speak English and Spanish—or only Spanish—Mass is offered at certain times in Spanish and other times in English.

The Roa children speak Spanish with their parents. Among themselves and outside the home, however, the three children speak English. Of the three, Karen's Spanish is the best. Because she heard only Spanish for the first years of her life, she developed a strong base in the language. Eskarleth, on the other hand, speaks Spanish with an accent. "Sometimes when I speak Spanish, I forget a few words and I have to say them in English. I don't talk Spanish that much, so my main language is English," she explains. Edgar, Jr., has grown up hearing Spanish from his parents, English from his sisters, and both languages at school and in his community. Because he has less experience than his sisters speaking Spanish, he has the most difficulty with the language.

After church the Roas often go to lunch at a nearby *fritanga*, a restaurant that serves typical Nicaraguan food, cafeteria style. Eskarleth's favorite dish is *repochetas* (soft corn tortillas wrapped around beans and melted cheese). At home Fatima cooks many of the same foods, but it's a treat to eat the *queso frito* (fried cheese) and *gallo pinto* (red beans and rice mixed together) at the restaurant. "Oh, and the desserts!" Eskarleth boasts. "If you haven't tried *tres leches* [a dessertlike pudding], then you haven't tried anything."

 In August 1993, Eskarleth and Edgar, Jr., visited their grandparents in Nicaragua. Three years earlier, Nicaragua had held the first free and fair elections in its history. Violeta Chamorro, the wife of the murdered journalist Pedro Joaquín Chamorro, defeated President Daniel Ortega, the Sandinista candidate. It appeared that democracy had taken a big step in Nicaragua.

Fighting and bloodshed had not stopped, however. In the Miami newspaper, the Roas read about sporadic contra attacks in Nicaragua. But Fatima's mother was sick. "I was thinking, What if she dies and never knows her grandchildren?" Fatima remembers. "*Ay, Dios, pobrecita* [Oh, my goodness, the poor thing]. They just had to go."

For years Eskarleth had heard stories about this faraway country where her parents were born and grew up. Now she would see it for herself.

Violeta Chamorro was inaugurated as president of Nicaragua in 1990. She served until 1996.

Eskarleth and her brother traveled together to visit their mother's parents in Managua in 1993.

Francisco and Thelma Ayala, Eskarleth's grandparents, live in a typical Managua home made of cement blocks. Some floors are tiled, but most are made of cement. The tiles and cement don't hold heat, which helps to cool the house. An overhanging roof connects the house to the bathroom. Cloth curtains, not doors, cover the doorways to the bedrooms. Electric fans cool the rooms, and mosquito nets over the beds keep the bugs at bay at night. The house has a big backyard with fruit trees and vegetables. Most families grow some of their own food.

Eskarleth remembers, "I thought my grandma knew everybody in Managua. Everywhere we went people said 'Hello, Hello, Doña Thelma.' And there, you see all the doors open, the gates open, and no bars on the windows. You hardly see any kids inside. They're all outside. And almost everybody walks to school. I hardly saw anybody in cars."

In Nicaragua Eskarleth observed that children her age usually wore just shorts and T-shirts. "They don't have a fashion in Nicaragua. Everybody just wears what they find in the closet," Eskarleth says.

One afternoon she went to eat at a small restaurant on the outskirts of town with her grandmother. "As soon as you come [into the restaurant], you see the monkeys all around. They're chained, but they swing all through the trees in the park next door. The door is open and the windows, too, so you can see all the deer and monkeys and other animals outside. Then this monkey came out. He didn't take the order but did sometimes take your food. It's adorable," Eskarleth says, her braces showing through a wide smile.

Eskarleth and her brother returned to Miami *encantados* (thrilled) with their visit. After all it was summer, and school was out. Besides that, well, their grandparents bent a lot of the rules usually enforced at home. But aside from all the fun, Eskarleth returned very affected, even confused, by what she had seen.

She told Fatima, "Mommy, even the little kids work there. They go around in the street selling things, oranges. They're so dirty. The children were asking me for food, for something to eat."

Fatima explained, "They're poor, Eskarleth. They have to do what they can."

Managua's many homeless street kids had a big impact on Eskarleth.

PAGAR UNA PROMESA (PAYING A PROMISE)

When Nicaraguans face a problem that seems too difficult to handle alone, it is common to ask one of the Catholic religion's many saints or the Virgin Mary (an important Christian figure) for help. In return, those asking for help must pagar una promesa, *or pay a promise. The promise is usually a service or a good deed, such as helping poor people or other unfortunates. The tradition of paying promises is a mix of the Roman Catholic religion—the major faith in Nicaragua —and the beliefs of local native peoples.*

When Edgar Roa had known Fatima for only a few months, he was seriously injured in a car accident one night on the outskirts of Managua. He nearly lost his eye, and his other injuries were so severe that doctors feared he might not live. Even if he did live, the doctors said, he probably would not regain consciousness.

Edgar's mother prayed for him. She prayed to God. And she prayed to Saint Sebastian—the patron saint of Diriamba (a nearby village) and the name of the Roas' neighborhood in Nicaragua. If only you will cure my son, she promised Saint Sebastian, he will pay a promise when he is well. My son will make *chicha* [a delicious local beverage made from fruit] and offer it to the whole village during the Saint Sebastian Festival.

Edgar not only lived and regained consciousness, he recuperated fully from the accident. His mother was amazed, grateful, and sure that Saint Sebastian had helped in this miracle. She told Edgar about the promise he must pay.

On January 20, the day of the annual Saint Sebastian Festival, Edgar rose early and headed to the kitchen of his home. He spent the early hours squeezing the juice from the fruit, swirling in sugar, and adding ice to the large barrel of chicha. When he was finished, he hoisted the barrel on his back. He spent the day under the broiling sun, walking through the festival. Whenever he met someone who looked especially thirsty—perhaps a poor person or a beggar—he offered them a cool drink. Each time he would say a blessing to Saint Sebastian. At the end of the day, Edgar was sweaty and exhausted, but he rested well that night. He had paid his promise to the patron saint.

Many Nicaraguans who have come to the United States no longer follow this tradition, but some still do. Since they moved to Miami, the Roas have only twice paid a promise. When Eskarleth was four years old, she developed juvenile arthritis, a crippling illness that can sometimes kill children. Please make her well again, Fatima prayed to her saint. Fatima promised to pay if her daughter was cured. When Eskarleth got better, Fatima and the whole family drove together—as she had promised—to pray and to give thanks at a church.

The second time the Roas paid a promise in the United States was after they received legal residency. The family had waited years for this. Fatima had promised long ago that if she and her family were granted their wish for residency,

she would return to Nicaragua as her payment. She promised to provide food for prisoners at one of the jails in Managua. In late March 1997, she returned to Nicaragua to pay her promise.

Participants in a street festival in Diriamba, Nicaragua, wear bright, colorful costumes.

One incident made a lasting impression on Eskarleth. She and Edgar, Jr., were taking a bus ride together. Eskarleth describes what happened. "When the bus stopped, this little boy hopped right on and grabbed Edgar's cap. The boy took a woman's necklace, too, then ran off." Eskarleth was surprised that the bus driver did nothing.

"The driver acted like nothing had happened. I'd *seen* stealing on TV and had heard about it, but I'd never seen anything like that. In Nicaragua they don't

Managua has many outdoor markets. People without refrigerators often shop daily for fresh fruits, vegetables, and other foods.

have as much security there. My grandmother told me later, 'If you have a necklace, keep it in your pocket. If they don't see it, they won't take it.'"

Despite the theft on the bus, Eskarleth liked how most people in Nicaragua feel safe enough to leave their doors open, even at night. She remarks, too, that even the dogs in Nicaragua seemed friendly.

"In a way, I liked Nicaragua, but in a way I didn't. It takes a lot of getting used to. It's very different from Miami. You have more things to do in Miami, so once you live here, you can't get used to it over there. In Managua there's not one single mall. There's like a flea market but a little bit better. I liked Nicaragua and would go again to visit, but not to live," Eskarleth sums up.

When they fled Nicaragua, Edgar and Fatima left everything—job, home, friends, and family. In the United States, they worked hard and sacrificed. Each year, like tens of thousands of other Nicaraguans in the United States, they had to fill out papers to work legally and to remain in the country. And each year, after weeks of anxious waiting, they were relieved to receive permission to stay. But Edgar and Fatima also knew that U.S.

This girl takes part in Miami's Santo Domingo de Guzmán festival celebrating the founder of the Dominican order of Catholic monks.

Edgar, Jr., practices dribbling on the family patio.

immigration laws can change. At any time, a new law might pass that could force the family to return to Nicaragua. Late at night, Edgar and Fatima would share their worries with one another. "What if we are sent back to Nicaragua?" But they never shared their concerns with the children.

"The girls would watch the news about Nicaragua and see the guns and fighting and be scared," Fatima says. "Edgar and I would talk, 'How could we go back there with the three children?' We'd hear about Nicaraguans [in the United States] being sent back. Ay, it was a huge worry.

"None of the children ever asked to go back to live," Fatima continues. "When Eskarleth and Junior visited, they were thrilled because they had an unforgettable vacation. But what they saw there was so much dust and dirty-faced kids."

Eskarleth says, "We never talked about going back that much, and when we did, we didn't talk about what it would be like living there. Mom just wanted us to stay here because there are more opportunities for us. That's all we talked about—our futures."

On May 28, 1996, the Roas climbed into their van and headed off to the Metro-Dade Justice building in downtown Miami. On the way, they stopped at Good Shepherd Catholic Church to pray and to ask for blessings.

In the courtroom, U.S. immigration judge Teofilo Chapa glanced through the thick folder containing the family's documents and history. He saw that the Roas had lived in the United States for a little more than 12 years—much longer than the 7 years U.S. law requires for families to stay permanently. Judge Chapa noted that Edgar had paid his taxes ever since he'd started working in the United States. Edgar owed no money and had never been in any trouble with the law. He saw that Edgar was president of the Association of Nicaraguan Engineers and Architects, a community organization that meets often with Miami area politicians. And the judge reviewed the recommendation letters showing what a well-respected member of the community Edgar was. Judge Chapa turned to Karen and asked about her grades. Satisfied with her good marks, he asked her if she had anything to say.

"I can't go back to Nicaragua," Karen replied respectfully. "I was raised in this country. I want to be someone, and everything that has to do with Nicaragua is in conflict." The judge nodded and looked to the prosecutor (the lawyer for the U.S. government). "Anything else to say about this family?" he asked.

The prosecutor had nothing to add. He didn't oppose awarding the Roas legal resident status so they could live permanently in the United States. He recognized that Eskarleth and Edgar, Jr., were both U.S. citizens because they were born in the United States. The family met all the legal requirements. And they were a strong, successful family that would benefit the United States.

"I want to welcome you as legal residents in this country," Judge Chapa said to the family and smiled. With his pen, he signed the order officially granting the family resident status.

Karen testified in front of a U.S. immigration judge in Miami.

Edgar's identification card is stapled to a document issued by the U.S. Department of Justice granting him and his family permanent legal residence in the United States.

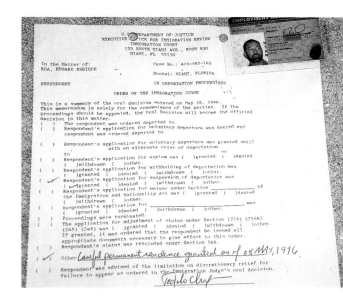

The Roas stopped at the first church they came to on their drive home. They don't even remember the name of it. They kneeled together on the cushioned front pew and silently said prayers. The many anxious years of waiting were finally over.

The Roas received their residency partly because they had proved to an immigration judge that they are an exemplary family. But tens of thousands of other Nicaraguans in the United States have not been as fortunate. To help these people, Edgar joined the Fraternidad Nicaragüense (Nicaraguan Fraternity), a group working to attain permanent legal status for most Nicaraguans in the United States. Edgar has traveled with the group to Washington, D.C. There he met with leading U.S. senators and representatives, hoping to convince them to pass legislation allowing other Nicaraguans to remain legally in this country.

In Miami Edgar meets periodically with Florida's government leaders. He has met Nicaragua's former president Violeta Chamorro, who visited Miami in the early 1990s. (Arnoldo Alemán was elected president of Nicaragua in 1996.) For his efforts to help other Nicaraguans, Edgar received a congratulatory letter from the Speaker of the U.S. House of Representatives.

As a young man in Nicaragua, Edgar was not politically active. But, he explains, "The circumstances of my life have brought me little by little into politics, not only for Nicaraguan issues, but also into politics in the United States." He laughs and adds, "I'm neither Republican nor Democrat—I've only just received my residency."

Edgar reflects, "Our family is happy today because we have been able to overcome almost all those problems we had when we first arrived—money, our legal status, and the [English] language. Now that the children are a little older, they're going about finding out what they want to do, and they all want to make something of themselves.

"The plan is that they will all get their degrees from college. Eskarleth wants to be a pediatrician [children's doctor]. Karen, too, wants to be a doctor. *Si Dios quiere* [if God is willing], we'll have two doctors in the family," he continues. "Little Edgar says he wants to be a pilot. We'll see."

Over the years, Edgar and Fatima have shared many worries about the safety and the future of their family.

Edgar and Fatima plan to become U.S. citizens soon. They often remind their children of their opportunities and of the difficulties they escaped. "The political situation in Nicaragua was so unsure. We came here to give the children a better chance," Fatima says. "Edgar and I sacrificed so that they could make something of their lives." Fatima continues, "We tell them, 'You have to make something of yourselves. Remember that always. You have to do the best that you can and carry the name of your country high so people will see the best of Nicaragua.'"

Karen, Eskarleth, and Edgar, Jr., lounge together on the couch. They have many plans for the future.

FURTHER READING

Cerar, Melissa K. *Teenage Refugees from Nicaragua Speak Out.* New York: Rosen Publishing, 1995.

Cummins, Ronnie. *Nicaragua.* Milwaukee: Gareth Stevens Children's Books, 1990.

Daniel, Jamie. *Nicaragua Is My Home.* Milwaukee: Gareth Stevens Children's Books, 1992.

Kott, Jennifer. *Nicaragua.* New York: Marshall Cavendish, 1995.

Nicaragua in Pictures. Minneapolis: Lerner Publications Company, 1993.

Rohmer, Harriet. *The Invisible Hunters (Los cazadores invisibles): A Legend from the Miskito Indians of Nicaragua.* San Francisco: Children's Book Press, 1987.

Rohmer, Harriet. *Mother Scorpion Country (La tierra de la Madre Escorpión): A Legend from the Miskito Indians of Nicaragua.* San Francisco: Children's Book Press, 1987.

PRONUNCIATION GUIDE

Chamorro, Pedro Joaquín (chah-MOHR-roh, PAY-droh wah-KEEN)
Frente Sandinista de Liberación Nacional (FREHN-tay sahn-dee-NEES-tah day lee-bay-rah-SYOHN nahs-yoh-NAHL)
Hernández de Córdoba, Francisco (ehr-NAHN-days day KOHR-doh-bah, frahn-SEES-koh)
Managua (muh-NAH-gwuh)
Nicaragua (nih-kuh-RAH-gwuh)
Roa, Eskarleth Arianne, (ROH-uh, ehs-KAR-leht ah-ree-AHN)
Sandino, Augusto César (sahn-DEE-noh, ow-GOO-stoh SAY-sahr)
Somoza Debayle, Anastasio (soh-MOH-sah day-BY-lay, ahn-ahs-TAHS-yoh)

Spanish Words and Phrases
chicha (CHEE-chuh)
encantados (ehn-kahn-TAH-dohs)
fincas (FEENG-kuhs)
fritanga (free-TAHN-guh)
gallo pinto (GUH-yoh PEEN-toh)
gusano (goo-SAH-noh)
maduros (mah-DOO-rohs)
pagar una promesa (pah-GAHR OO-nah proh-MAY-suh)
pasteles (pah-STEHL-ays)
pobrecita (poh-bray-SEE-tah)
queso frito (KAY-soh FREE-toh)
repochetas (ray-poh-CHEHT-uhs)
si Dios quiere (SEE DEE-ohs kee-EH-ray)

INDEX

ABOUT THE AUTHOR

Michael R. Malone is a writer, journalist, and teacher living in Miami. He writes both in Spanish and in English on issues of culture and ethnicity in the Americas. His articles have appeared in the *New York Times,* the *Washington Post,* the *Miami Herald,* and EFE, the international news wire agency of Spain. He has interpreted, translated, and researched for *Frontline* television documentaries and for several books on Latin America. His first children's book, *Journey Between Two Worlds: A Guatemalan Family,* was selected as A Notable Children's Trade Book in the Field of Social Studies for 1997.

PHOTO ACKNOWLEDGMENTS

Cover photographs by © Tina Gue/Panos Pictures (left) and Michael R. Malone (right). All inside photos by Michael R. Malone except the following: © Gino Russo, p. 6; © Brian Vikander, pp. 7, 15, 20, 34, 37, 51, 54; © Bill Gentile/ZUMA, pp. 8 (top), 9, 10, 13, 17, 28, 32, 49, 53; © Etchart/Impact/ZUMA, p. 39 (right); Professor Daniele Di Piazza, pp. 8 (bottom), 31; Independent Picture Service, p. 23; Frederica Georgia, p. 35; UPI/Corbis-Bettmann, pp. 12, 24, 26; © Tina Gue/Panos Pictures, p. 14; Roa Family, pp. 16, 39 (left); © Archive Photos/ Gerald Davis, p. 25. Mural cut-ins by Michael R. Malone. All artwork and maps by Laura Westlund.

ALL ABOUT

The way

WE LIVE

ALL ABOUT

The way

WE LIVE

DP

DEMPSEY
PARR

Author
Francesca Baines

Designers
Diane Clouting and Phil Kay

Editor
Linda Sonntag

Project Management
Raje Airey and Liz Dalby

Artwork Commissioning
Susanne Grant

Picture Research
Kate Miles and Janice Bracken

Additional editorial help from
Lesley Cartlidge and Libbe Mella

First published in 1999 by Dempsey Parr
Dempsey Parr is an imprint of Parragon
Parragon, Queen Street House, 4 Queen Street, Bath, BA1 1HE, UK

Copyright © Parragon 1999

Produced by Miles Kelly Publishing Ltd
Bardfield Centre, Great Bardfield, Essex, England CM7 4SL

ISBN 1-84084-460-4 (Hardback)
ISBN 1-84084-481-7 (Paperback)

Printed in Italy

CONTENTS

THE WAY WE LIVE

ALL ABOUT THE WAY WE LIVE is divided
into fifteen different topics, each covered
by a double-page spread. On every spread,
you can find some or all of the following:

- Main text to introduce the topic
- The main illustration, designed to inform
  about an important aspect of the topic
- Smaller illustrations with captions, to
  describe aspects of the topic in detail
- Photographs of unusual or specialized
  subjects
- Fact boxes and charts, containing
  interesting nuggets of information
- Biography boxes, about the people who
  have influenced society
- Projects and activities

LANGUAGE

EVERY TIME YOU SPEAK you use a complicated system of sounds called a language. A language is a way of organizing the sounds to communicate information and ideas. We use language in so many ways it is impossible to imagine a world without it. Language helps us to describe how we feel, to talk to other people and to learn about them. Finding words for objects and ideas also helps us to make sense of the world. There are probably between 5,000 and 6,000 different languages in the world today. English is spoken by around 1.4 billion people, but many other languages are used by just a few hundred people. The languages we use today have taken thousands of years to develop, and they are still changing so that we can describe new ideas, inventions, and discoveries.

Language and identity

People feel very strongly about the language they speak. Your language is part of who you are, your history and culture, and people protest strongly if another language is imposed upon them. In some countries, where more than one language is used, there are laws to ensure that one language is not given second place to another. Road signs in Canada, for example, must give information in French before English.

In Israel, street signs appear in Arabic and in English. This sign in Bethlehem must be one of the most photographed in the world

Groups of languages

Although the languages of Europe may sound very different, they have many features in common and are probably all part of the same language family. The root of this family is a language known as Indo-European. Indo-European is also the root of languages in areas of southern Russia, Iran, Afghanistan, Pakistan, and northern India. The similarities between these groups of languages could mean that many thousands of years ago tribes from northern Europe moved south into Asia. Over the centuries Indo-European developed into the many different languages spoken in these countries today, but certain words and structures remain the same.

A common language binds people into communities who share a similar cultural history and outlook on life

Latin

Latin was the language of the Romans, whose civilization dominated Europe around 2,000 years ago. Although Latin has not been a living language for centuries, it has continued to be used as a common language in many areas of learning, such as science. There are millions of different species of plants, for example, but biologists all over the world can be sure that they are talking about exactly the same species because they have an international "master" list of names. On the left is the passionflower, in Latin, *Passiflora Kermesina*.

We use gestures to signify agreement and anger, as well as to direct someone's attention

Sign language

People who are deaf communicate using a language of hand signs. Some signs represent whole words or ideas, such as "hungry," or "animal", other words have to be spelled out using the sign for each letter of the alphabet.

Body language

It is often not just the words that matter when you speak, but the way you say them and the signals you give with other parts of your body, such as the expression on your face or the gesture of a hand. Body language is particularly important when you greet someone, but you have to be careful because, like spoken language, it is often different from country to country. And sometimes body language can cause real confusion. While in most of Europe you might signal "no" by shaking your head, in India a shake of the head from side to side means "yes."

Tower of Babel

According to the Book of Genesis in the Old Testament of the Bible, the Tower of Babel was built in Babylon with the aim of reaching all the way from Earth to heaven. The god of the Old Testament was angry that people should so arrogantly presume they could get to heaven, and punished them by confusing the language of the builders. This resulted in chaos, and the tower was never completed. Today the word "babel" means a confusion of noises and voices.

Dying languages

It is impossible to give an accurate figure for the number of languages there are in the world. As people explore the world and discover new communities, they find new languages. But languages are also disappearing. When more widely spoken languages are introduced into remote communities the native language often becomes forgotten. A quarter of the world's languages have fewer than 1,000 speakers—often just a hundred or so people—and these languages will almost certainly disappear over the course of the next 50 years.

ESPERANTO

In 1889 an artificial language called Esperanto was invented by Ludwig Zamenhof. His idea was to create an international language that would be easy for everyone to learn. Esperanto is used at meetings of international organizations, like the United Nations, and is taught in many schools. There are journals and newspapers in Esperanto, radio broadcasts in Esperanto and the Bible and the Qur'an are among many books translated into that language, but it has not yet been recognized, due to opposition from groups who want English to be accepted as the world language.

WRITING

WRITING IS A WAY of recording information and passing it on to others. Without the writing of ancient peoples, we would know very little about the history of the world. Today, writing is just as important. It allows us to keep in touch through newspapers and the Internet. Writing can take different forms. Pictograms use a sequence of pictures to communicate information. Ideograms use marks called characters to describe abstract ideas, such as "sorrow." Other scripts, called alphabets, use characters to represent a sound, and create words by putting the sounds together. There are five different alphabets used in the world today: Greek, Roman, Cyrillic, Hebrew, and Arabic. The European languages, such as English and French, use the Roman alphabet. Russian and related languages use the Cyrillic alphabet. The advantage of the alphabet system is that you have to learn only a few signs to be able to read—the 26 characters of the Roman alphabet used in English, for example. With a system that uses pictograms and ideograms, you may have to learn symbols for each of thousands of different words, as in Chinese.

The history of writing

The first writing was probably invented around 5,000 years ago by the Sumerian people of Mesopotamia, which is today part of Iraq. It was called cuneiform, which means "wedge-shaped," because it was written by pressing a reed into soft clay tablets to make wedge-shaped marks. Cuneiform writing started off as pictures of objects, called pictograms. But over time, the pictures were simplified to make them quicker to write. Chinese writing dates back to around 1500 BC. Chinese used ideograms and sound signs as well as pictograms, and was written using a brush and ink. At around the same time as the Chinese started writing, the Egyptians began to use hieroglyphs—a mix of pictograms and sounds. The Egyptians wrote with reed brushes or pens on papyrus—a type of thick paper made from the stems of the papyrus plant. When papyrus ran out, it was replaced by parchment made from animal skins. Paper from wood pulp was first made by the Chinese in AD 105. Alphabetic script was first invented by the Greeks around 100 BC.

Scribes

In ancient Egypt, scribes were very important people. Their training took up to 12 years and enabled them to get jobs as teachers, librarians, or civil servants. In the Middle Ages, all books were handmade by scribes. They illuminated, or decorated, the initial capital letters on a page. They used real gold and silver, as well as inks in many colors. They often used a red lead called minium, which led to small pictures being called miniatures. To copy a book might be a lifetime's work for a scribe.

For many centuries very few people could read or write. Documents were written by hand by a scribe. Books were so valuable that they were often chained to a library desk to stop them from being stolen

This reed pen and baked clay inkpot date from biblical times. Reed pens were easily made with a knife, but wore out quickly

Roman writing tools

The Romans used a metal stylus to inscribe words on to a soft wax tablet. The writing could be rubbed out with the flat end of the stylus and the tablet used again. For writing on papyrus, the Romans used ink made from soot mixed with water. Their ink wells were of clay or stone.

PUNCTUATION

When you are reading text it is important to know where one sentence begins and ends, and where to pause in the sentence. To help make sense of writing, languages have their own system of marks, called punctuation, which shows the reader how the words hang together.

The text on the Rosetta stone is a thank-you to a ruler of ancient Egypt

Unknown scripts

There are still ancient scripts that experts are not able to understand. Egyptian hieroglyphs would probably still be a mystery if it were not for the discovery of the Rosetta Stone in 1799. On this ancient stone, the same piece is written in three different languages. By comparing the Greek words with the hieroglyphs a Frenchman named Jean-François Champollion was able to work out the meaning of the hieroglyphs.

Computers

The language of computers is a series of numbers that is practically impossible for a human brain to understand. The computer program translates the operator's instructions into the machine code that is used inside the computer. It then translates the computer's responses back into the language that the operator can understand. All this happens in a split second.

Arabic

The Arabic alphabet has 28 letters. Seventeen basic characters represent the consonants. Eleven dots were added later in the history of the script for the vowel sounds. The curved characters are written from right to left. Arabic script was probably first used in the 4th century AD. It spread with the rise of the Islamic faith, and was widely used by the 7th century AD. The holy book of Islam, the Qu'ran, says that writing is a gift from God and calligraphy (the art of artistic writing) is highly respected.

АБВГДЕЖЗИ
ЙКЛМНОПР
СТУФХЦЧШ
ЩЪЬЬЭЮЯ

Chinese

Chinese is a very complex written language with more than 50,000 characters, which are a mix of pictograms, ideograms, and sounds. These have hardly changed for centuries, and the Chinese have little trouble reading ancient scripts. At school a Chinese child will learn around 4,000 characters. The strokes of each character must be made in the right order, and some characters are made up of 26 different

Russian

The Russian alphabet is called Cyrillic. It is based on the Greek alphabet of the 9th century AD, but gets its name from St. Cyril, a churchman of that time who preached the Christian faith to the Slavonic people. The Slavs lived in the area of modern-day Russia, Poland, Bulgaria, the Czech and Slovak Republics, and Serbia. The Cyrillic alphabet is used to write Bulgarian and Serbian as well as Russian.

WRITE YOUR OWN PICTOGRAMS

You can make your own writing system using pictograms. You could invent pictograms that would be easy for anyone to read, or devise a trickier system that only you and your friends could understand. See if you can read the secret message above. It's an invitation to meet under the tree at midday to go for a day's fishing, then eat the fish for dinner as the sun starts to go down. Why not start off by writing your own invitation, perhaps to go bowling or skating?

MYTHS AND LEGENDS

MYTHS AND LEGENDS are tales of gods and goddesses, monsters and heroes. But they are also stories that explain the many mysteries of life, such as how life began, what happens when we die or why the Sun rises at dawn and sets at dusk. As well as explaining life, myths teach the rules of life—good triumphs over evil, and weaknesses like greed or vanity are always punished. Many myths have survived for thousands of years, passed down by word of mouth, or in pictures and written words, and these shared stories bind communities together. Every culture of the world has its own myths, and although the stories they tell are very different, they often have the same themes. Legends are different from myths in that they are thought to have some basis in historical fact and to tell of real people. But as they are told over the centuries, the details of the legend are exaggerated and elements of magic may be added to make the story more colorful.

Monsters

Myths are full of fabulous beasts and dreadful monsters. Dragons of all shapes and sizes appear in many mythologies. In most cultures dragons represent the forces of evil that must be overcome, but in Chinese mythology, dragons represent good fortune.

The phoenix

The phoenix was a mythical Greek bird, with shimmering feathers of gold and bright colors. Believed by some to have a life cycle of exactly 500 years, the phoenix is a symbol of immortality and renewal. When the old phoenix reached the end of its life, it would burn itself on a funeral pyre. A young bird would then rise from the flames in its place. The young phoenix would fly with its father to the altar of the Sun god in the Egyptian city of the Sun, which the Greeks called Heliopolis.

The young phoenix rises from the flames of its father's funeral pyre

Creation myths

All over the world, people have tried to explain how the world began and where the first people came from. The Ancient Egyptians believed that at the dawn of time Ra, the Sun god, created the air, moisture, the earth and the sky, and that humans came from his tears. In Norse tradition it is said that the earth was created by the mighty god Odin and his brothers from the flesh of the frost giant that they had killed. They made rocks and stones from his bones, and rivers, lakes, and oceans from his blood, and people were created from logs. In Chinese mythology, at the beginning of time there was chaos, which was shaped like an egg. From the egg came yin and yang—the opposite forces of light and dark, male and female, hot and cold—that make up the universe. Out of the egg, too, came P'an-ku, the first being, and he created the Earth and everything in it. The aboriginal people of Australia believe that life was created in the Dreamtime—a time before time. In the Dreamtime the eternal ancestors awoke from their sleep to wander the Earth and transform plants and animals into human beings, before going back to sleep.

This stone carving shows the head of Quetzalcoatl, the Aztec serpent god

Quetzalcoatl

Quetzalcoatl was the Aztec god of creation, learning, and the winds. The Aztecs said that as god of the winds, he came to sweep the way for the rains that would bring fertility to the earth. The winds made the vegetation of the earth sway like a serpent covered with green feathers.

Sacred places

The most sacred place of the aboriginal people is a huge rock in central Australia, called Uluru (Ayers Rock). The aboriginals believe that their ancestors live in eternity. They call this time before time the Dreamtime. In the Dreamtime the ancestors walk the land along paths known as song lines and all the song lines meet at Uluru.

Sedna, ruler of the sea, lives with her father and dog-husband in the depths of the ocean. She is both sea goddess and goddess of the dead

A cunning trickster

The Ashanti people of West Africa have many stories of Ananse the spider. Small and seemingly powerless, she was in fact creator of the world and can outwit any animal, including the lion, python, and leopard. When the Ashanti were taken as slaves to America, the legend of Ananse combined with Native American stories of the trickster Great Rabbit, and the Brer Rabbit stories were born.

The goddess Sedna

The sea was the source of food for the Inuit people of Greenland and northern Canada. Sedna the sea goddess was worshipped for the sea creatures she provided to eat. She was also feared in case she was offended and made the Arctic weather so harsh that hunting and fishing for bears, seals, and whales became impossible.

Uluru is the most sacred place of the aboriginal people of Australia

Charon, the ferryman crosses the river Styx, escorting the dead to the afterlife

Death and the afterlife

Perhaps the greatest mystery of all is what happens to us when we die. The ancient Greeks believed that the souls of the dead traveled to the Underworld, which they called Hades. To get there they had to cross the river Styx with the help of Charon the ferryman. To ensure that the dead reached the Underworld they were buried with a small coin, which would be used in the afterlife to pay Charon.

WAS KING ARTHUR REAL?

The legend of the English King Arthur and the Knights of the Round Table is full of mystery and magic, but it is believed that the real Arthur was a brave Celtic chieftain who lived around AD 500. The first tales of him were written in Latin by monks in the Middle Ages. Among the best known is the one in which he pulled the sword from the stone.

LITERATURE

LITERATURE IS THE ART OF WRITING. It is more than writing just to convey information, it is writing to entertain, to stir the heart, and to explore all sorts of human experience. It offers the best chance we ever get of feeling what it is like to be someone else. Writing is only counted as literature if it stands the test of time. If a piece is really well written and expresses a deep truth it will still be read many years later, and in translation all round the world. There are many different literary forms —stories, novels, poetry, plays, biographies, diaries, and journalism. Made-up stories are called fiction, and feature the same themes the world over—adventure, crime, love, horror, and fantasy. The events a fiction writer describes are called the plot. The people who take part in the plot are called the characters. The best fiction writers create characters so true to life you feel they are real people. Non fiction writers may record the lives of great men and women and the effect of historic events. Literature is also an important place for exploring new ideas, for trying to influence politics, and for protesting injustice.

The first stories

Stories were not always written. They were first told around the fires of cave dwellers, and then passed down by word of mouth through the generations. Each storyteller developed more interesting details and twists of the plot, so the tales grew richer and more vivid with every telling. The tradition of storytelling is called the oral (spoken) tradition. When writing was developed, stories could be written down, but for many centuries only a very few people could read or write, and books had to be written or printed by hand. In the royal courts of Europe singing storytellers, called bards, were employed to write and recite stories and poems. Today in the developed world almost everyone learns to read, and printing technology means that books are inexpensive, but the oral tradition continues everywhere as people tell each other the stories of their own families and communities.

Alongside singing, music and the antics of a jester, storytelling was a popular form of entertainment in the medieval banqueting hall

Epic poems

Great legendary heroes have often been celebrated in long poems, called epics (or sagas). At first these poems were not written down, and would have been sung or recited. One of the most famous epics is the Anglo-Saxon poem of Beowulf, a legendary prince who kills Grendel, the man-eating monster who lives in the marshes, and then kills Grendel's mother.

Left, a manuscript of Beowulf. Below, a still from The Thousand and One Nights

Great classics

Great stories are still read many years after they were first invented. The Thousand and One Nights is a collection of Middle Eastern stories believed to be 2,000 years old. The tales are told by Queen Scheherazade, whose husband wants to kill her. She puts off her death each night by telling him a wonderful tale, such as the story of Sinbad the Sailor. After 1,001 nights of stories, he agrees to spare her life.

Poetry

Poetry is a very careful arrangement of words that gives them special meaning. Some poetry rhymes, but much does not. There are many different forms of poetry: a sonnet is a poem with 14 lines, a Japanese haiku is a verse with just 17 syllables. Often poets write about very intense emotions, but poetry is also written simply to entertain and amuse.

This Japanese painting of cherry blossom against distant misty mountains echoes the simplicity of the haiku. In just a few words, the Japanese poet puts the reader inside his own emotions

The first books for children

It is only in the last 300 years that books have been written especially for children. Until then children simply listened to folk tales and fables. The first important works for children appeared in the 19th century, when Hans Christian Andersen and the Brothers Grimm produced their collections of folk and fairy tales. They were followed by adventure stories, such as *Treasure Island* by Robert Louis Stevenson, and fantasies, such as *Alice in Wonderland* by Lewis Carroll.

Above, The Princess and the Pea, a tale told by Hans Christian Andersen. Left, Tenniel was the illustrator of Alice in Wonderland

THE POWER OF BOOKS

Throughout history writers have challenged old ideas and explored new lines of thought, and books have proved an important influence on public opinion. In 1850 Harriet Beecher Stowe wrote *Uncle Tom's Cabin*, a novel that describes the evils of slavery in the United States. The book played an important part in bringing slavery to an end. But books that criticize governments are sometimes banned or burned and can get the author into trouble. In 1974 the Russian writer Alexander Solzhenitsyn was exiled for his criticism of his country's regime.

THEATER

FOR THOUSANDS OF YEARS people have enjoyed bringing stories to life by acting them out. The first performances were probably ritual dances by ancient peoples calling upon the spirits to help them and using dance, music, make up, and costume to add force to their message. Today, plays or stories are usually performed by actors in a theater—a building specially designed for dramatic shows. In the grandest theaters the stage is overlooked by rows and rows of seats so that a large audience can watch the performance. There is a large area behind the stage for scenery, and an area where the orchestra can sit so that live music can accompany the performance. Special lights hung around the stage help to create the atmosphere. Many people work in a large theater, designing and making the scenery and costumes and preparing the actors for the show. But actors can be just as entertaining when performing plays in a small open space with a few simple props.

Below is one of the most magnificent theaters of ancient Greece, the theater of Herod Atticus, built on the Acropolis at Athens. In ancient times actors would play several parts in a drama, changing masks to show which character was speaking. Left are the masks of comedy and tragedy

Greek theater

The earliest theaters that survive today are the open-air Greek theatres built about 2,300 years ago. The actors performed on a stage at the center—an area called the orchestra—and the audience sat in a semi circle around them on rows of stone seats. The clever design of the theater meant that the actors' voices carried clearly to the back rows. Behind the orchestra was an area for costumes and props. The actors were all men and they wore masks depicting a range of set characters, including women.

Puppet shows

Not all plays are performed by human actors. Puppet theater is very popular all over the world and involves figures that appear to come to life when moved by a human operator. Puppetry dates from at least the 5th century BC. There are many different types of puppet. Glove puppets are worn on the hand, string puppets (sometimes known as marionettes) are operated from above, and rod puppets are operated from below. Punch and Judy shows, a favorite seaside entertainment in Britain, feature glove puppets representing a husband and wife who are always arguing and fighting. Another type of puppet is the string puppet. In Indonesia there are Wayang Kulit shadow puppets. The characters are cut out of leather and their movement is controlled with metal rods. An oil lamp behind the puppets makes their shadows fall on to a screen on which they act out traditional stories. The audience sits in front of the screen and watches the shadow play. Shows usually last many hours and being a puppet master is very demanding work. He not only operates the puppets, he narrates the story, conducts the musicians and may also play an instrument himself.

Shadow puppets are popular throughout Southeast Asia. They are made of leather and moved from beneath by means of metal rods. A light behind them throws their shadows on to a screen, beyond which the audience sits to watch the drama

Traveling theater

The 10th century saw the rise of Christian religious drama in Europe. Actors took to the road and traveled around performing in the street or in the courtyards of inns. Often the stage was simply the back of the actors' cart. The audience would gather and put money into a hat that was passed around. The actors performed mystery plays, which told stories from the Bible and, later on, morality plays about the battle of good against evil. Some plays were performed in episodes over a number of days.

The townspeople call out their encouragement as good and evil do battle

Pantomime

In Britain, pantomimes are plays with music and dancing. They began with the Italian Commedia dell'Arte, traveling players of the 16th century, who told the traditional love story of Harlequin and Columbine. Today the shows take a well-known fairy story such as Cinderella, Aladdin, or Red Riding Hood and incorporate a range of different acts—such as clowns, singing, and magic. The tales are comic and usually feature an "Old Dame"—a foolish, ugly, old woman who is played by a man dressed as a woman.

Frenchman Marcel Marceau, one of the most famous mime artists of all time

Japanese Kabuki theater

The popular theater of Japan is called Kabuki. It originated in the 1600s and still plays to packed houses. The shows are lighthearted with lots of singing and dancing, and are performed on an unusual stage with a bridge that runs through the audience, called the flower walk. The actors, who are all men, wear highly decorative costumes, dramatic stylized make up, and wigs that reveal the personalities of the character they are playing.

Mime

Mime is a form of silent theater. There is usually a musical accompaniment, but the actor does not speak at all. Instead, he or she tells a story using vividly accurate actions and expressions. The art of mime reached a new high in the 20th century with the great French artist, Marcel Marceau.

THEATRICAL MAKE UP

Make up can help actors to convince an audience of their character. Learn how by making yourself up with face paints. Try out different roles, such as villain or clown, and see if you can make yourself look old by adding wrinkles and lines. Then turn yourself into an animal! Does make up change your character?

DANCE

PEOPLE ALL OVER THE WORLD love to move their bodies to the rhythm of music—to dance. People dance for many different reasons. The first dances were probably part of rituals, religious worship, and magic. Because dancing is beautiful to watch as well as to perform, it became an entertainment that rich people paid to see, and dancers are known to have performed at the courts of the pharaohs of Ancient Egypt. Dances can also be a powerful form of storytelling. The Maori people of New Zealand use dance to teach their children about their history. Today, many forms of dance are regarded as art. Many of the classical or traditional dances of the world can be performed only by professional dancers who have been specially trained in the correct movements. But there will always be dancing just for fun, that can be enjoyed by anyone who wants to join in.

Ritual dance

Dance plays an important part in the rituals or ceremonies of many cultures. The Mbuti children of Africa must learn special dances before they can become adults. Ritual dances are also performed to calm angry spirits or to drive out evil ones. In Sri Lanka when someone is sick a "devil dance" is performed to rid the body of the demons believed to be causing the sickness. The Aborigines of Australia dance around a magic stone to bring rain, and many of the Native American tribes of North America have traditional war dances that were once performed to prepare the men for battle and call upon the spirits to help them.

Young Mbuti people from Zaire decorate their bodies with white make up for a dance to celebrate the beginning of adulthood

Religious dance

Kathkali is a sacred Hindu dance of India in which the performers act out the stories of their gods. Every movement and gesture the dancer makes is important, even eye movements. The dancers wear bright costumes and dramatic head dresses, and dance to the music of drums. Singers with cymbals and a gong act as narrators. The stories usually concern the chaos brought about by human weaknesses until harmony is restored by the gods, and performances often go on all night.

Today kathkali dancing (left) is often performed for the benefit of tourists. But to the Hindu audience and players, it still has strong religious significance

Flamenco dancers of Spain wear tight dresses that flare out into swirling multi tiered skirts

Ballet

Ballet is a theatrical form of dance that began in the French court in the 16th century. Over the centuries ballet dancers have perfected a repertoire of classical techniques and movements, which they use to tell stories. Some of the best known are the romantic ballets of the 19th century, *Swan Lake*, *The Nutcracker*, and *Sleeping Beauty*. The music for these three ballets was composed by Tchaikovsky.

Folk dance

The traditional dances of ordinary people are called folk dances. Flamenco is the national folk dance of Spain. It is performed in spectacular dress to guitar music, singing, and clapping. Flamenco has a very dramatic and emotional style— the dancers stand straight and proud, stamp their feet and click their fingers to the rhythm, and shout out to encourage each other. Some dancers shake and tap a tambourine as they move, and others play castanets—wooden clappers held in either hand. Like other folk dances, flamenco can be performed anywhere— outside in a town square or in a bar.

These ballet dancers perform a pas-de-deux, a traditional romantic sequence for the hero and heroine of the story

ICE DANCING

Ice skating is an Olympic sport as well as a popular entertainment. The craze for ice dancing reached its peak during the 1980s with the gold medal-winning partnership of Jayne Torvill and Christopher Dean. The pair revolutionized their sport by inventing dance sequences with spectacular movements that built up into a story. You may have wondered why skating looks so graceful. The whole weight of the skater is concentrated on the small area of skate that touches the ground—the narrow blade. The enormous pressure under the blade melts the ice, and this reduces friction, so that the skater can glide along.

Ballroom dancing

In the 17th century, while the ordinary people of Europe met at folk dances, the nobility went to balls to dance the minuet. Today the formal dance style lives on as ballroom dancing. The most popular ballroom dance is the waltz. Once a peasant dance from southern Germany, it was considered shocking when first introduced into 18th-century ballrooms, because couples had to dance so close together. The tango (right) calls for even closer contact.

In modern dancing, anything goes. Clubbers dance to a frenetic beat and repetitive trance-like music. Some club owners go to extraordinary lengths to surprise their members, including filling the dance hall with foam!

Jive

New forms of music often inspire new ways to dance. In the 1940s, American jazz bands began playing exciting new kinds of music called swing and boogie-woogie. New energetic dances had to be invented to keep pace with the music. One technique, called jiving or jitterbugging, was particularly wild and demanded stamina as well as perfect timing. Men swung their partners around and around, slid them along the floor between their legs, and flung them high up into the air!

DANCE STEPS

These footprints show the basic steps of the waltz. It will help to count to the beat: "one, two, three, one, two, three, one, two, three…," stressing the 'one' every time as you zigzag around the room. The second step in each section should move to the side, and not be a straightforward walking step. As you relax into the rhythm and start to move more freely, allow your body to sway away from the reaching foot and toward the closing foot. If you step on your partner's toes, don't worry!

MUSIC

MUSIC IS SIMPLY A PATTERN of sounds that is good to listen to. These sounds can be arranged in many different ways to produce music in a wide range of styles, including classical, jazz, pop, or folk. Every culture in the world has its own distinctive tradition of music and song, often played on unique local instruments. But all music is a form of expression—a way to communicate feelings both happy and sad. In particular, people can express their feelings together through music. Today crowds at sporting events often chant spontaneously with excitement to encourage their team, as in the past slaves laboring in the fields sang together, inventing words and music to keep up a working rhythm and rally their downcast spirits. Music was probably first used in primitive religions, to communicate with the gods and to please them. It is still part of the ritual of most of the major religions today. Music was first written down in the form of notes by monks of the 9th century AD. Before then, all music was learned by listening and repetition. But the discovery of ancient instruments, paintings, and written descriptions do give some idea of how it sounded.

Traditional instruments

Many countries and regions of the world have their own unique musical traditions. The music played by the local people of an area is called folk music, and it is often played on traditional instruments. The aboriginals of Australia have an instrument called a didgeridoo, made from a long straight branch that has been buried in the ground until it is eaten hollow by ant like insects called termites. The didgeridoo makes a low droning noise and is played at night-time ceremonies, called corroborees, when aboriginals gather around a fire to sing, dance and play music.

The didgeridoo is a heavy instrument that has to be played resting on the ground

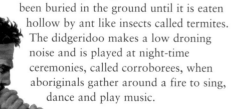

Melody, rhythm, and harmony

Music is made up of sounds, called notes, organized into a pattern that people find pleasing. These patterns are made up of three different elements—melody, rhythm, and harmony. The melody is the tune, a pattern of notes in a certain order. It is the part of the music that you recognize and remember. Rhythm is marked by a steady beat—the beat that you follow if you clap or dance to a tune. Harmony is the mixing together of notes to make a more interesting sound. When one person sings a tune there is no harmony, but two voices or a choir can sing different notes at the same time to make a rich harmony of sound.

MOZART

Wolfgang Amadeus Mozart (1756–1791) was born in Austria, the son of a violinist and composer. From a very young age Mozart showed extraordinary musical talent. He began composing when he was five, and at six he started to travel around Europe performing harpsichord concerts. As an adult, Mozart made his home in Vienna, where he taught and composed. He wrote a total of 600 pieces in his life, including 41 symphonies, 27 piano concertos, and many great operas, such as The Magic Flute and Don Giovanni. Although today he is known as one of the greatest composers ever, he died a poor man at the age of just 35.

String instruments

String instruments are played by making stretched strings vibrate. This can be done by drawing a bow over them, as with a violin (left) or cello, or plucking or strumming the strings, as with a guitar. The shorter the string, the higher the note played. The player makes different notes by pressing the string down on to a fingerboard and shortening it. The sitar is a string instrument from India. It has up to seven strings, as well as 12 secondary strings that create a background drone.

Wind instruments

The family of instruments that are blown to make sound are called wind instruments, and include woodwind instruments, such as the clarinet and saxophone, and brass instruments, such as the trumpet and the French horn (left). Woodwind instruments were originally all tubes made of wood, although some today are made of metal. Their sound is made by either blowing across the mouthpiece or over a thin strip of wood in the mouthpiece, called a reed, which vibrates. Different notes are made by opening and closing holes along the tube with your fingers, which alters the length of the tube. Brass instruments are tubes of metal curled round so they are not too long and unmanageable. Notes are usually made by pressing valves to alter how far down the tube the air travels. In the trombone, however, this is done by moving a sliding tube to alter the note.

Keyboard instruments

The piano is a keyboard instrument. When you press a key it works like a lever to make a felt-covered hammer hit strings to sound a note. A grand piano (above) has its set of strings laid out horizontally. An upright piano is more compact because its strings are arranged vertically. The piano was originally called the pianoforte, which means soft-loud in Italian, because it can be played very quietly, or make a sound powerful enough to fill a concert hall.

Percussion

The simplest musical instruments are percussion instruments, such as drums, triangles, and xylophones. Percussion instruments are struck, either by hand or with a beater, to make sound. There are hundreds of different percussion instruments, often specific to different regions of the world and made of local materials. Traditional African music has a strong rhythm beaten out on drums.

How many of these instruments do you recognize? They are, from left to right, xylophone, violin, trumpet, clarinet, percussion, and double bass

RADIO AND TELEVISION

IN 1901 GUGLIELMO MARCONI first sent signals across the Atlantic using electromagnetic (radio) waves. Radio waves carry information about sound and—as it was later discovered—pictures, and radio and television were born. Up until then news travelled slowly. You could only communicate with distant friends or family by letter or telegraph. National news broke only as quickly as the newspapers could be printed and distributed. In remote areas of the country national events could pass people by unnoticed. The advent of radio and television meant that everyone could be informed about and involved in the events of the country and the world as they happened. Broadcasters have enormous power because they control the flow of information. The way they report the news can also affect people's opinions. But radio and television can also offer unique access to information and entertainment, enabling you to follow the World Series, or events in a remote rain forest.

How television reaches your home

Television programs are broadcast to homes using radio waves carrying signals about sound and pictures. These signals can reach your home in several different ways. They can be broadcast over a local area from a tall transmission mast to rooftop television antennas. Programs can also be broadcast over long distances using satellites in space. A television signal is transmitted into space from a large dish antenna, called an Earth station. The satellite picks up the signal, amplifies it and sends it back to Earth. Satellite signals can be picked up by a small dish antenna pointing directly at the satellite. Television signals can also reach homes via underground cables. The cable is made up of dozens of fiber-optic cables as thin as a hair, each carrying one channel.

How a television set works

A television set receives radio signals carrying separate information about sound and pictures. Sound signals travel straight to a loudspeaker. Picture signals are sent to the picture tube (known as a cathode ray tube). Here beams of electrons (parts of atoms) are fired at the inside surface of the screen. The screen is made up of thousands of dots of chemicals, called phosphors, which glow either red, blue, or green. Combinations of dots build up a full colour picture. Seen in quick succession—25 to 30 pictures per second—the images give the impression of movement.

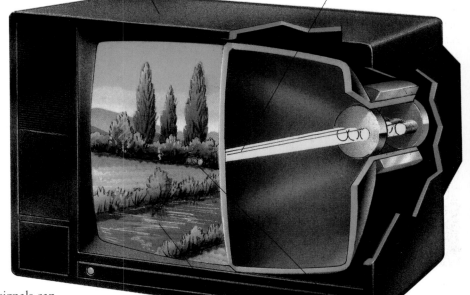

A TV set receives electric signals, which it changes into pictures and sound

Streams of particles are fired on to the back of the screen

The picture changes many times a second, giving the effect of movement

The streams of particles build up a picture

Signal is beamed up from transmitter to satellite

Signal is beamed back from space to tv mast

Signal travels from television studio

Signal arrives inside tv set in your home

Guglielmo Marconi (1874–1937) was the Italian scientist who developed long-distance radio broadcasting, and laid the foundations for television transmission. He started experimenting with radio waves in 1894, aiming to invent a system that would send messages in Morse Code over long distances without the use of wires. By 1899 he had achieved a transmission of 8 miles (14 km) across the Bristol Channel in England. By 1901 he had sent messages from Cornwall in England to Newfoundland on the other side of the Atlantic Ocean.

Outside broadcast

To get the most up-to-date news stories, television reporters often have to film outside the studio at the scene of the action. For a really big story crews are linked directly to the studio with an outside broadcast unit in a van or truck that has a transmitter. A simple news story can be covered by just two people, a reporter and a camera operator using a video camera.

Inside a studio

Most television programs are made in a studio. Here the actors, or a host, stand on a set (stage) surrounded by cameras, microphones and lights. The camera crew wear headphones linking them to a control room. Monitors in the control room show exactly what is happening on the set, so the different material can be co ordinated for transmission.

How a radio works

A radio set is a radio wave receiver that uses an antenna to pick up the signals broadcast from a radio transmitter. Radio waves travel at different speeds, known as wavelengths or frequencies. Radio stations broadcast each channel using a different frequency, and a tuner on the radio set allows you to select the station you want. An electric circuit in the radio set turns the waves into electronic signals to make sound, and an amplifier makes these sounds louder.

This selection of old radios—now collectors' items—shows how radio design and technology has changed. Many radios today incorporate a CD player as well as a tape deck

Digital versus analog technology

In a digital system information is represented by electrical pulses, instead of smoothly changing electric signals, which are analog. Digital pulses represent numbers, which in turn can represent any type of information, including sound and pictures. Digital systems use only two numbers, zero and one, which combine in a code.

SOUND-EFFECTS

When a radio drama is recorded the actors read a script into a microphone while a sound-effects technician makes noises to give an impression of the activity or setting. Sound effects are simple to create at home. Try recording a story with the help of some friends using some of the sound effects below and see how they add to the atmosphere. A ghost story is particularly good for this purpose.

For footsteps on the path, fill a tray with gravel and step up and down on it. For a horse's hooves, knock together two empty coconut shells. (An old trick, but it's really convincing!) To make rain, pour water from a watering can on to a tin tray (preferably outside, or over a sink!). For thunder and lightning, experiment with tin trays and a wooden spoon. Bashing a tin tray creates a really good effect, especially if you have a tray that shudders when you shake it. For wind, simply blow into a jar.

PHOTOGRAPHY AND CINEMA

PHOTOGRAPHY allows us to capture significant moments in our lives in still images and has filled the world with moving pictures through motion pictures (movies) and television. The camera is a sealed box that allows no light in, except when the shutter at the front opens and you take a photograph. The light reflected by the object in front of the camera passes through the lens, which focuses the light on to a piece of film. The film is a type of plastic coated with chemicals that are sensitive to light. In black-and-white photography there is just one layer of these chemicals, but in color photography there are three layers, each one sensitive to either blue, green, or red. Together, these primary colors make up the full range of colors that we can see. Light alters the chemicals on the film and when the film is developed, the image created by the light is fixed and a picture is revealed, but the light and dark areas are reversed. This is called the negative. Projecting the negative on to light-sensitive paper produces a print with the dark and light areas the right way round.

Moving pictures

Moving pictures—or movies as we know them today—became possible when George Eastman invented flexible film in 1889. Pictures could be taken in quick succession and when projected at speed the images merged to give the impression of movement. The first movie was shown in Paris in 1895. Early films were silent and in black and white. Music accompanied the story and words appeared on the screen to help the audience follow the plot. Movie actors such as Charlie Chaplin and Rudolph Valentino became stars. In 1927 it became possible to record sound with pictures and in 1932 films were first made in color. Over the decades techniques have continued to advance and movie making is now a popular multi million dollar entertainment business.

Making a movie

Making a motion picture usually begins with a producer. The producer chooses the storyline and finds the money to film it, picks the director and other technical teams, and plans the making of the film. On the set the director is in charge of the large teams of people involved in production. He or she directs the actors and makes the creative decisions that will give the film its character. The set is designed by an art director, a cinematographer is responsible for the cameras, there are sound and lighting crews and many others.

Putting a film together

Once a film has been shot the different individual sequences must be put together in the right order and combined with a soundtrack. This is done by a film editor, who works closely with the director to tell the story in the best way. The editor's choice of which pieces of film to show and what to leave out can affect the character of a film, by building up the suspense, altering the audience's understanding of the plot, or speeding up the drama.

Special effects

Part of the magic of cinema is the special effects than enable a director to recreate dramatic action sequences, such as accidents and catastrophes, and fantasy worlds populated by dinosaurs.

MOVIES IN INDIA

India is the biggest movie-going nation in the world. Around 9 million movie tickets are sold each day, and more than 700 full-length feature films are made each year. Most Indian films are action-packed and full of romance, singing, and dancing, and are made in Bombay—also known as Bollywood. Every Indian city and town is full of cinemas, and traveling movie vans visit remote rural areas.

Hollywood

American film making took off at the beginning of this century in a small town outside Los Angeles called Hollywood. The sunny climate meant films could be made all year round. Today Hollywood is the home of the big American film studios (film-making companies) and of many glamorous film stars. Every year, the stars gather at a glittering ceremony, when Academy Awards (or Oscars) are given for achievement in the film industry.

Animation

Animation is the art of bringing drawings or models to life in film. Cartoons are made by filming a sequence of drawings—at least 12 per second—to give the impression of movement. Today computers are able to draw the pictures linking one action to another, making animated films quicker and cheaper to produce. Clay models are animated by repositioning the characters minutely between each frame (individual shot).

Modeling skills can be important in animation

SIMPLE ANIMATION

You can bring a drawing to life by making a flick book. Take a drawing pad or notebook and, starting at the back, draw a character in the top right-hand corner. You don't have to be good at drawing for this to work, a stick person will do. Decide what your character is going to do—walk, jump, or turn a cartwheel, for example.
Then on the next page draw the same character a little further on in their activity, so that you end up with a sequence of between 12 and 20 pictures. Then use your thumb to flick slowly through the pages and watch your character move.

PAINTING AND SCULPTURE

PEOPLE HAVE ALWAYS enjoyed expressing themselves through painting, but they have also painted to record important events or famous people, or simply to decorate their homes or public places. When you look at a painting it is not just the subject matter that is interesting, often it is style that the artist has used—it might be simple or highly detailed, natural, or romanticized. It might be a lifelike representation of a scene or the forms may have been changed or distorted. Painters are constantly experimenting with painting materials, giving paintings new textures and forms. Sculpture is three-dimensional art, so as well as looking at it you can often touch and feel and walk around it. There are two basic techniques for making sculptures: either a solid block—often made of stone or wood—is carved out, or liquid metal is poured into a mold, called a cast.

How colors react with each other

You can experiment with colors by painting squares of different colors, cutting them out and placing them next to each other in different combinations. Notice how the colors change character. Putting black next to white makes the black more black and the white more white. If you put very different colours together, such as green and red, the same effect is achieved. If you put similar colors together, such as blue and violet, the colors will appear to jump and merge in a quite exciting way.

Red, yellow and blue are the primary pigments. Red mixed with blue gives purple. Red mixed with yellow gives orange. Yellow mixes with blue to give green.

Painting materials

The first paintings were done on cave walls using sticks and natural pigments. Today most painters use brushes to apply their paint, but the paints themselves have changed little over the centuries. Pigments or colors may come from berries, bark, roots and earth, shells, beetles or even metals. They can be mixed with a vegetable oil, to make oil paints, or with water to create watercolors. Oil paint is used on canvas, and is very versatile—it can be used thickly or thinly and built up in layers, and produces strong colours that last a long time.

Watercolors are made from pigment dissolved in water, and are used to paint on paper, which absorbs the color. Watercolors are easy to apply, dry quickly and can be mixed with varying amounts of water to create either strong or light colors.

Artists at work in a studio. A constant light source is important to painters. As the sun goes around from east to west it distorts both colour and form, so a good studio has windows facing north, which get no direct sunlight, and "artificial daylight" lighting for duller days

COLLAGE

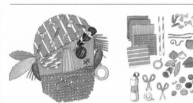

A collage is a picture made up of a combination of materials—paints, different qualities of paper stuck one on top of the other, or any other materials that you think would help to create the effect you are after—printed papers such as newspaper, straws, pieces of fabric, bits of string, and even pasta. Try making a collage portrait of yourself (or make a collage of an animal), using as many different textures as you can.

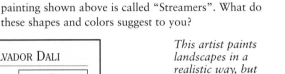

Abstract art

The word abstract means something that does not have any recognizable shape or form. In the 20th century the term abstract art was first used to describe the paintings of artists who painted ideas rather than objects or scenes. The Swiss artist Paul Klee explored ideas such as harmony, rhythm, and shape in his works. The painting shown above is called "Streamers". What do these shapes and colors suggest to you?

Looking at pictures

Before the invention of the camera, painting was, and still is, used to record important events or people. Portraits of famous people usually show them in a setting that explains who they were and why they were important. Often, portrait painters had to make their subjects look better than they did in real life. Paintings are often historical documents that show what people wore or ate, their social standing, the jobs they did and how they spent their leisure time.

This artist paints landscapes in a realistic way, but includes abstract shapes that produce a disturbing effect

Most artists prefer to mix paints from a tube on a palette (below, on the bench) so they can arrive at their own more subtle colors. Artists' brushes are very expensive items and need to be cleaned and stored carefully after use. The sculptor uses a lump hammer and a flat chisel to put the finishing touches to her work

SALVADOR DALI

Salvador Dali was a Spanish artist who lived from 1904 to 1989. He was an expert draftsman and used a smooth, clean painting technique, but he is best known for the extraordinary subject matter of his paintings. Dali was one of the leaders of the Surrealist painting movement of the early 20th century. These were painters who wanted to show a world outside the real one ("sur-real" means above the real). Dali filled his work with startling images from his dreams and fantasies, such as a telephone in the shape of a lobster and melting watches hanging limply over a wall.

This discus thrower carved from marble is a Roman copy of a Greek sculpture from 450 BC

Carved sculpture

Carved sculpture is made using chisels and hammers to cut away at a solid block of material. The most common materials are stone, especially marble, and wood. Often the sculptor makes a small model, called a maquette, before embarking on the actual sculpture. The next job is to carve the rough shape, cutting the block with a chisel and hammer. The detail is carved with hand chisels and fine scrapers. Finally, both wood and stone may be polished to give the sculpture a smooth texture.

British sculptor Henry Moore used both stone and bronze. His two-piece reclining figure cast in bronze (below) can be seen in Germany

Cast sculpture

There are many different stages in making a cast sculpture. First, a rough of the sculpture is made from clay. This is covered in a layer of wax, on to which the sculptor can carve the fine detail. Then the whole thing is covered in a layer of heat-resistant plaster with holes at the top and bottom to make a mold. Molten metal is poured into the mold, taking the place of the wax, which melts and runs away. The metal cools, then the mold is cracked open to reveal the culpture.

BUILDINGS

FROM SIMPLE HOMES to mighty monuments, bridges and tunnels, buildings are designed to make life easier, safer, or simply more interesting. All buildings have one thing in common—they were constructed for a specific purpose. In a sports stadium thousands of people must all be able to get a good view of the action. A bridge must get people from one side of a divide to the other. A cathedral must reflect the glory of god, with soaring spires, glowing stained-glass windows, and a chamber that resonates with singing and prayer. Building techniques have evolved over the centuries, but much remains timeless, such as the purity of Ancient Greek temples, the beauty of natural materials including wood and marble, and the simple practicality of nomad tents in the Sahara.

Çatal Hüyük in Turkey had buildings of mud brick, with flat roofs and narrow streets

Mud huts and grain stores are built around a yard or compound in this Dogon village in Mali, Africa

Building materials

Homes can be made out of almost anything. The first shelters were made simply out of available natural materials, such as mud, straw, wood, stone, ice, leaves, grass, and animal skins, as it was impractical to carry materials far. People began building with bricks around 6,000 years ago, at first using blocks of earth that they dried in the sun. Later, they discovered that baking the bricks at high temperatures made them lighter, stronger, and longer-lasting. Today a wide range of building materials is available, including reinforced concrete (concrete around a steel framework), iron, steel, bricks and glass. Sometimes, however, traditional local materials are still the cheapest and most practical alternative. These Dogon huts in Mali, Africa, are made from mud and straw.

BUILDING FACTS

● The limited technical equipment of the builders of the past, compared with the lifting and digging machines available today, did not stop the construction of the awe-inspiring pyramids of ancient Egypt or the European cathedrals of the Middle Ages.

● The biggest cities in the world are in Japan, where large cities have spread and joined up to make giant cities. Japan is made up of islands with high mountains, so most people live on flat strips of land around the coast. To grow, cities have to spread out like ribbons until they finally merge into each other. More than 27 million people live in and around Japan's capital city, Tokyo.

Homes for people

The first people were nomads, who either sheltered in caves or lived in portable homes such as tents made from animal hides. But when people learned to farm they settled down and built more permanent homes. The style of homes varies greatly all over the world, and is determined mainly by climate and local building materials. As communities grow they find different ways for large numbers of people to live together. Today, one solution is to build tall apartment blocks. In 7000 BC in the town of Çatal Hüyük (now in Turkey), 6,000 people lived side by side in homes built of wooden frames and mud bricks. To save on space and building materials, the houses were built one against the other, sharing walls, with few streets between them. The doors were in the roof, and a ladder led down into the living area. This kept the houses cool and kept out animals. It also had the advantage of making the town difficult for a potential enemy to capture.

Classical architecture

The Ancient Greeks and Romans admired buildings that displayed balance, proportion, and simplicity. Today this style is known as classical architecture. The Parthenon in Athens, Greece (440–431 BC), is a good example of classical Greek architecture with rows of columns supporting a triangular roof. Three orders of Greek architecture are Doric (plain-topped pillars), Corinthian (pillars decorated with foliage, left), and Ionic (ram's horn pillars, right).

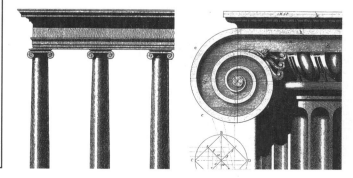

Towns first grew up when people learned to farm. They no longer had to run after herds of wild animals for their food

Islamic architecture

The traditional architecture of Islamic countries is influenced by the Muslim religion, and the mosque is not only the place where people worship, but the building at the heart of any community. Mosques often have a simple outline with a central dome, which Muslims believe to be the most perfect shape on earth. They also have towers called minarets, from which people are called to prayer. According to Islamic law, buildings cannot be decorated with images of living things. Instead ceramic tiles and mosaics are used to create geometric designs, or they are decorated using calligraphy (the art of writing). Arches are another common feature of Islamic design, with many variations on the basic horseshoe arch.

A dome decorated with geometric patterns is a classic feature of Islamic architecture

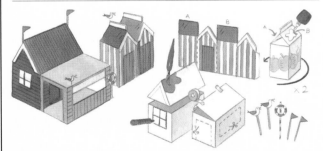

MODEL BUILDING

Collect cereal boxes, shoeboxes, and cardboard to build a series of beach huts for your window sill. You can cut out the walls and roof in one go, to make the hut stronger. For a square hut, the front, back, and two sides should be equal upright rectangles. The front and back need a triangle added on for the roof pitch. The tabs for the roof should be as tall as the height of the pitch. Cut out the hut, stick it together from the inside with tape, then paint the roof red and paint the walls with stripes of bright color.

Skyscrapers

Toward the end of the 19th century, advances in building technology, new materials, and the invention of the elevator made it possible to construct buildings taller than ever before. The first skyscrapers were built in Chicago, Illinois, in the 1880s. They soon became status symbols for American companies and grew taller and taller. The skyline of Manhattan in New York (below), is dominated by skyscrapers. The Chrysler building was completed in 1929 as a symbol of the greatness of the American automobile manufacturer. The Empire State Building, built in 1931, was for some time the tallest building in New York, with a height of 1,246 feet (380 m). This record was broken in 1972 by the World Trade Centre, which is 1,374 feet (419 m) tall.

WORLD RELIGIONS

OUR LIVES ARE FULL of questions, many of which are very hard to answer. Why are we born? Why do we die? How did the world come into being? Why is there unhappiness and suffering in the world as well as joy and love? Religions are sets of ideas and beliefs that try to make sense of these mysteries. In many cases, they also offer principles by which people should live their lives. The first religions were spirit religions dedicated to the many spirits or gods of nature. Spirit religions were not written down, but used stories and myths to explain the world. Today there are many different religions, each with its own god or gods. Three of the major religions—Islam, Christianity, and Judaism—believe in only one god. The fourth, Hinduism, has many gods. The principles of these religions are set down in sacred texts—the Christian Bible, the Qur'an of Islam, the Jewish Talmud and Torah, and the Hindu Vedas. Of the thousands of other religions throughout the world, whether institutionalized or private and personal, many share very similar forms of worship – prayer, meditation, singing, and chanting.

At Easter Spanish Christians commemorate the last journey of Jesus before his crucifixion by walking in procession through the streets. Often an effigy of Jesus on the cross is carried at the head of the procession

The wearer takes on the spirit embodied in this wooden African mask

Spirit religions

The first religions were based on the worship of the spirits or gods of the natural world—in the animals, plants, rivers, and mountains. These are called animist religions and they are traditional religions passed down by word of mouth. Animist religions are still practiced all over the world. The people of the Amazon rain forest believe in the spirits of the trees and creatures of the forest they live in, but respect the powerful spirit of the jaguar above all others. Each of the Native American peoples has its own individual religion, but they all share the belief in the great spirit who created the Earth and the spirit in every natural thing. Peoples in the northwestern United States carve animals on totem poles to protect them.

Christianity

Christians are the followers of Jesus Christ, a preacher who lived 2,000 years ago in Palestine in the Middle East (now Israel and Palestine). But many people were suspicious of Jesus and his teachings and while still a young man he was arrested and crucified (hung on a cross to die). Three days after his death his tomb was found empty and he appeared to his followers several times before he finally ascended into heaven. Christians believe that Jesus was the son of God and that he died to release people from their sins. There are 2 billion Christians living all over the world today and many different branches of Christianity. The most important Christian festivals are Christmas, which celebrates the birth of Jesus, and Easter, which celebrates Jesus rising from the dead. The symbol of Christianity is the crucifix (cross) on which Jesus Christ died.

Islam

The religion of Islam began 1,400 years ago in the city of Mecca (now in Saudi Arabia) when Allah (the Muslim name for god), spoke to Muhammad the prophet. Muhammad wrote down Allah's words in the holy book, the Qu'ran. Islam means submission, and the followers of Islam, called Muslims, submit themselves to Allah's will and try to live in a way that is pleasing to him. When they die, Muslims believe that they are judged and sent to either heaven or hell. Today more than 900 million Muslims live all over the world but mostly in the Middle East, Asia, and Africa. Muslims pray five times a day facing toward Mecca, but can worship anywhere, even in the street. All Muslims must try to make a pilgrimage (called a Haj) to the holy city of Mecca once in their lives.

RELIGIOUS WARS

Throughout history religion has been the cause of many long and bitter wars. Some conflicts have started as disputes over sacred sites. The city of Jerusalem, for example, lies today in the Jewish state of Israel, but it is also a holy city for Muslims and Christians. As a result it has been a hotbed of violence for centuries. Strongly held religious beliefs can also result in intolerance of other religions. Conflict between Muslims and Hindus caused the partition (division) of India in 1947 into the Hindu state of India and the Muslim states of Pakistan and, later, Bangladesh.

Judaism

Judaism began around 4,000 years ago in the Middle East. The Jewish people are descended from the nomadic Hebrews who finally settled in Canaan (now Israel), the land that God had promised them. Throughout their history, the Jews have repeatedly been forced out of the promised land and into exile, and today they live scattered around the world in what is called the diaspora. Jews believe in one god and work toward a just and peaceful life for everyone on earth. They also believe that God will send the world a Messiah to bring peace and harmony. The Jewish holy day is the Sabbath, which runs from sunset on Friday to nightfall on Saturday. This is a day of rest and worship when Jews attend a service in a synagogue.

Hinduism

Hinduism began in India around 5,000 years ago and is one of the oldest religions. Today there are around 733 million Hindus, mostly living in Asia. Hindus believe in a supreme soul or spirit without form, called Brahaman. There are many other Hindu gods, but they all represent different aspects of Brahaman's power and character. The three main gods are Brahma the creator, Vishnu the preserver or protector, and Shiva the destroyer. Hindus believe that when you die your soul is reborn in another body as a person or an animal. This is called the cycle of rebirth, and your actions in this life influence what you become in the next life. Every Hindu seeks to live a good life so that their soul can break out of this cycle and join with the Brahaman. There are many Hindu festivals and celebrations but the main ones are Diwali, Holi, and Dusserah. Diwali is a festival of light in late October or early November. Holi is a spring festival when Hindus worship the Lord Krishna. Dusserah is a celebration of the triumph of good over evil, and in South India it is marked by setting fire to a giant paper statue of the demon Ravana.

Hindus look forward to new beginnings at Diwali by putting welcoming lights in their windows, doors, and temples and wearing bright clothes to celebrate the triumph of good over evil, and light over dark

Buddhism

Buddhism was founded by Siddhartha Gautama, a royal prince born in Nepal in 563 BC. Unhappy with life, Siddhartha spent many years praying and meditating until he gained enlightenment and finally understood the truths of life. He was given the title Buddha, meaning awakening or enlightenment. Buddhists do not believe in a god but live their lives according to the teachings of the Buddha, following the middle path between luxury and hardship. They believe that after death they are reborn and that the way they live decides whether the next life will be better or worse. Their aim is to escape the cycle of rebirth and find a state of happiness and peace, called nirvana. Most Buddhists today live in Asia, but Buddhism is also practiced in Western countries.

Chinese ancestor worship

Around 5 million people in China and the Far East follow Confucianism. This religion is based on the teachings of Confucius (left), who was born in 551 BC in China, and who dedicated his life to teaching people how to live in peace and harmony. Confucius believed that the way to lead a better life was to respect other people and honour your ancestors. Children are taught to respect their parents and elders and to visit temples to worship their long-dead relatives.

FESTIVALS AND TRADITIONS

THE CELEBRATIONS, FESTIVALS, and traditions of the world are very varied, but what they all have in common is that they are occasions people share, and this both enriches the lives of the world's communities and makes them stronger. Many festivals offer the opportunity to dress up, dance, sing, tell stories, and eat traditional foods. But a festival can also be a solemn time for reflecting on important issues. Some occasions are part of the history of a country or community and mark a key event, such as the day a nation gained its independence or ended a war. Countries also commemorate the lives of important people, such as the great civil rights leader Martin Luther King, who is remembered each January in the United States. The world's religions have their own celebrations such as the Christian Christmas or the Hindu festival of Holi. Seasonal celebrations mark springtime and harvest, and bring light and warmth to the depths of winter. Festivals that are repeated regularly down the generations become traditions that everyone looks forward to.

New Year festivals

In Scotland the New Year begins at midnight on the first day of January, and is called Hogmanay. Scottish people hold hands in a circle, sing a song called "Auld Lang Syne," and wish each other good luck. For Jewish people, New Year is also a religious festival called Rosh Hashanah. They reflect on the things they have done wrong in the past and promise to do better in future. For the Chinese, New Year is a spring festival. People get together for a big meal and to exchange presents, and there are celebrations in the streets, with men dancing inside an enormous dragon costume. There may also be acrobats and jugglers, and firecrackers are exploded to frighten away evil spirits.

Corn dollies are woven in all sorts of shapes and are symbols of fertility

Religious festivals

Festivals are often an important part of religious celebrations. The most important event in the Christian year is Holy Week. It takes place in the spring and remembers the last week of Christ's life. Palm Sunday marks the day on which Christ entered Jerusalem riding a donkey, and people laid palm leaves in his path. Holy Thursday commemorates the last supper Christ ate with his followers, and Good Friday (meaning god's Friday) marks the day Christ died on the cross. The week ends on Easter Sunday, the day he rose from the dead. One of the most important Hindu festivals is Holi, which is also a spring festival of rebirth. As part of the celebrations, Hindu children throw colored powder and water over each other. This custom is particularly associated with Krishna, the playful young god.

Playful Hindus sprinkle each other with coloured powder to welcome spring

At the Chinese New Year people parade through the streets in a dragon skin

Harvest festivals

Harvest festivals are celebrated the world over to give thanks for a successful harvest. Thanksgiving in the United States is also an important part of remembring America's history. It echoes the first harvest celebration of the early settlers in Massachusetts. They survived only with the help of the Native American Indians who taught them to farm, to catch turkeys, and to find wild foods such as cranberries. Thanksgiving is still celebrated today with turkey and cranberry sauce. A harvest tradition in Britain is to make a corn dolly from the last sheaf of wheat to be cut, where the spirit of the corn is believed to be hiding. The dolly may be burned in the spring and its ashes scattered as the field is plowed, so returning the spirit of the corn to the soil and nourishing the earth. Every year in October the Germans celebrate the hops harvest with a beer festival. In Mexico they have a radish festival. On Christmas Eve the largest radishes are carved into shapes and set out to decorate restaurant tables

Marriage customs

Weddings are important celebrations marking the new beginning for two people. Promises are made, and family and other guests join in the well-wishing. Often weddings are religious ceremonies full of rituals and symbols. At a Hindu wedding there is always a sacred fire as a symbol of the presence of god and his wisdom. At a Jewish wedding the bride and groom drink from the same glass, then crush it underfoot to remind them that love is fragile and they must work hard to keep it. In both Jewish and Christian tradition rings are exchanged as symbols of the marriage. Rings are symbols of eternity, being circles with no beginning and no end, reminding the couple that they have pledged to love each other for ever.

A Children's Festival

● In Turkey, April 23 is Children's Day. A child even gets the chance to sit at the desk of the country's prime minister! There are puppet shows, dances and kite-flying competitions.

● In Japan, Children's Day is May 5. Paper kites in the shape of fish are hung from poles to stream in the wind.

Fasting

Not all special occasions are marked with meals and parties. Several important religious festivals are remembered with a period without food, known as a fast. The Jewish New Year is a solemn time when Jews remember the past and ask forgiveness. After nine days, the ceremonials are brought to an end with Yom Kippur, which is a day of fasting. The most important festival of the Muslim year is Ramadan. The Muslim holy book, the Qur'an, calls for all Muslims to fast from dawn to dusk for one month to commemorate the time when Allah gave his teachings to the prophet Muhammad. The end of Ramadan is celebrated with a special feast called Eid (below).

Seasonal festivals

The changing seasons are also an occasion to celebrate. In Sweden they celebrate the longest day of the year—Midsummer. People dress in traditional costume to dance and sing around a pole decorated with flowers and leaves. In northern Sweden the Sun does not set all night and celebrations go on right through till morning.

Remembrance

November 11 is Remembrance Day in Britain, when people remember those who died in the wars of this century. The day marks the end of World War I (1914–1918). Today paper poppies—a reminder of the poppies that grew on many of the battlefields of World War I—are sold to raise money for the families of those killed in that war, and the wars that have followed it. Wreaths of poppies are laid at a special memorial by the Queen and other important figures, and a two-minute silence is observed to remember those who gave their lives.

The Swedes celebrate Midsummer by dancing all night

GOVERNMENTS

IT IS NOT POSSIBLE to involve everyone in the decisions made every day in running a country. Instead a group of people, known as a government, make these decisions on behalf of the people. Governments have many responsibilities, including taxation, health care, education, defense, welfare, and environmental policy. A government's priorities and the way it runs the country are decided by the political views—the beliefs and ideas about running the country—of its members. There are many different ideas and theories about how this should be done, but people who share similar views group themselves into a political party. There are two main types of government: democratic government and autocratic government. In a democracy people are able to vote for the political party that best represents the views they hold about running the country. In an autocracy there are no elections, or there might only be one party and no choice of candidates.

Democracy

Countries where the people can choose their government are called democracies. At a general election each person puts a cross on a piece of paper to make their choice known. Then their votes are counted up to see who has won. India is the largest democracy in the world. Every adult citizen is able to vote for people to represent them in the national parliament. At the election in 1996 more than 343 million people voted out of a total electorate of more than 592 million. Organizing an election in India is extremely difficult. There are 15 different languages and 21 states, so there had to be 565,000 polling stations and 3 million polling officers.

More than 340 million out of a total of 590 million voters lined up to take part in India's 1996 general election

Monarchy

A monarchy is a country that is ruled, or a whose government is headed by a king or queen. In many traditions this right to rule was and still is believed to have been granted by God, and throughout history monarchs have had great power deciding the laws of the country and collecting taxes. A monarch's right to absolute power was first challenged by the people of France in the 18th century. In a series of events known as the French Revolution the people finally executed their king and France became a republic.
Today there are still many monarchs, but few have real power. These monarchs have a more diplomatic role, representing their country abroad or acting as figureheads at events of national importance.

The oba (king) of Akure wears traditional robes and a beaded crown for occasions of state. He is the ruler of the Yoruba people of Nigeria

GOVERNMENT FACTS

● The world's oldest parliament is in Iceland. Called the Althing, it was started by Viking settlers in AD 930.

● The people of ancient Athens, in Greece, started the first democratic assembly nearly 2,500 years ago. But it wasn't completely fair, because women and slaves weren't given the right to vote.

● Traditionally the king or queen of England owns all the swans on the River Thames, except for those marked in a special annual ceremony.

Dictatorship

In a dictatorship one person or group holds all the power and does not allow any opposition. The power might be held by an individual, a family, a political party, or a military group. From 1939 to 1975 Spain was a dictatorship, ruled by General Francisco Franco (right). He seized power after the country was divided by civil war, and succeeded with the help of the military in crushing all opposition. He continued to rule until his death in 1975.

Republic

A republic is a state, which means that it is not ruled by a monarch but by the people, who elect their government representatives and a head of state, such as a President. The United States of America is a republic and it is governed according to the Constitution (laws setting out how the country should be run), written in 1787. The Constitution sets out three branches of government: the President, Congress and the Supreme Court. The President leads the executive branch, which decides and carries out the government's policy. Congress makes the laws of the country and the Supreme Court makes judgments according to the law. The government was set up in this way to prevent any one branch becoming too powerful.

The White House in Washington, D.C., is the official residence of the President of the United States

Communism

The ideas of communism are based on the works of Karl Marx (1818–1883). Communism means "belonging to all" and Marx believed that working people would revolt against the ruling classes that exploited them, and together take ownership of everything. He held that people should work in cooperatives and share all goods and services. The communist party has ruled China since 1949 when Mao Zedong (1893–1976) took power. Although the regime has improved conditions of the mainly agricultural society of China, the powerful state government restricts the freedom of the individual.

This statue of heroic workers is one of many in communist North Korea

The United Nations

The United Nations (UN) is an organization dedicated to world peace. Most countries have a representative at the UN General Assembly, which meets in New York. The UN helps the world's governments to work together and sends peace-keeping troops to war zones and trouble spots.

Capitalism

A capitalist system is one that is based on the belief that those who have money or "capital" should be allowed to use it to generate more money. This might be done by starting up businesses or investing money in other businesses to allow them to generate more profit, which the investor takes a share of. The financial systems of many countries, such as France (below) are based on the general principal of capitalism, but rules and regulations are needed to keep this in check so that a rich minority is not allowed to exploit a poor majority.

NELSON MANDELA

Nelson Mandela (born 1918) was a South African lawyer. In 1948 South Africa adopted a policy called apartheid, which meant the segregation of the races, and rule by the white minority. Mandela joined a black nationalist party called the African National Congress (ANC), which opposed apartheid. In 1962 he was arrested and sentenced to life imprisonment. Throughout his 27 years in jail he continued to speak out against apartheid and became a symbol of the injustice of the regime. In 1990 Mandela was finally released, age 71. In a referendum in 1992 South Africans voted to end apartheid rule, and in 1994 Mandela was elected the first black president of South Africa.

TRADE AND MONEY

Trade is the exchange of goods and services—buying and selling. Coins were invented when overseas trading began and merchants used weights of precious metals, such as silver, to buy and sell. Overseas trade has shaped the world. When European traders found rich markets in foreign lands they made great efforts to protect their interests. Sea faring nations such as Britain, Portugal and Holland established colonies in distant lands with their own armies and police forces and so, through trade, built huge empires and became world powers. The world today survives on trade. Few countries are self-sufficient, so they sell what they have to raise money to buy what they need. Products are visible items such as food or automobiles, or "invisible" items such as the labor or manufacturing expertise that makes a product, or a financial service, such as insurance. In international trade today little actual money changes hands, as transactions take place on paper or over the telephone and are managed using computer systems.

Money

Money is a recognized form of payment. Today units of money are represented by notes and coins, but they have taken many other forms. Cowrie shells were once used in China, India, Thailand, and Africa. Other forms of money include copper rings, salt, beads, stone dishes, cocoa beans, and axes. When the first coins were issued, it was the weight that determined their value. Paper money was first used by the Chinese in the 10th century as an alternative to dealing with large quantities of metal coins. At first paper money was simply a handwritten receipt, but later receipts of fixed values were issued by governments.

Markets and bazaars

Markets are still at the heart of communities all over the world. Every day people travel to the village markets of India and Africa to buy and sell, to meet friends and exchange news. In Thailand there are floating markets, with vegetables, fruit, flowers, and spices being sold from boats called sampans. A bazaar sells craft goods. Moroccan bazaars are famous for their brassware (left).

Trade

Early people could make, find or grow most of the things they needed for everyday life, but as civilization developed and communities grew, people began to need more things. Craftsmen, such as potters or weapon-makers, developed businesses. Peddlers and local farmers would meet once a week at a market to sell their wares. The first permanent shops probably appeared in Europe in the Middle Ages, but they were only the front room of someone's house. People did not use money, but bartered or exchanged items they judged to be of equal value or worth—a quantity or wood, or food, an ax, or a day's labor. Today we calculate the value of something in terms of units of money, but the value of something may not be fixed, and haggling over prices is still very much part of buying things in markets the world over.

In an Indian street market, a trader waits for customers to buy her fresh produce

How trade shaped the world

The world as we know it today has been shaped by trade. The first so-called explorers were in fact traders sent on missions to find new trade routes, markets, and products. The Italian sailor, Christopher Columbus, who is credited with being the first European to reach America in the 15th century, was in fact on a mission to find a shorter trade route route from Europe to India and the East Indies, where valuable spices grew. Merchants also traveled a route called the Silk Road to bring back precious silks and porcelain from rich Chinese cities. They faced a grueling journey across the Gobi desert, through the mountains of Central Asia to trading ports in the Middle East, and around the Mediterranean Sea.

In Arabia, camels belonging to traveling merchants made long journeys across the desert laden with valuable goods to sell

Trade centers

Trade centers have traditionally grown up in places where transportation is good and there is no shortage of materials, goods or labor. The busiest and largest port in the world today is Rotterdam in the Netherlands. It thrives on its connections to the river Rhine and to the sea. A key center in the East is Hong Kong (left).

Imports and exports

The goods and services that a country sells abroad are its exports, and the goods and services that it buys in are its imports. Imports and exports are compared to calculate a balance of payment between two countries. If one country exports more to another country than it imports from it, it is said to have a trade surplus. If it imports more than it exports, that is called a trade deficit.

Containers are unloaded at Southampton Docks, UK

Stocks and shares

The initial cost of starting up a business is called the financial capital, and often this money is borrowed. The people who lend the money all hope to have a share in the company's profits in the future. The capital is divided into a number of shares, and each share has a certain value. This value may go up or down, depending on how the company performs. The only place shareholders may sell their shares (or a unit of shares called a stock) is through a Stock Exchange (right). Here they are traded (bought and sold) by a broker who is a member of the Stock Exchange.

MONEY FACTS

● A currency is a money system, such as the Japanese yen, the French franc, the US dollar, the Mongolian tugrik, or the Bhutan ngultrum. The exchange rate is what it costs to buy or sell one currency for another. This changes on a daily basis,

● The process of stamping a design on to a coin is called minting. One side of the coin usually shows the head of a famous person or the symbol of the body that guarantees the value of the coin. Only an authorized producer, known as a mint, is allowed to manufacture and stamp coins. Coins not made at a mint are forgeries.

INDEX

ACKNOWLEDGMENTS

The publishers wish to thank the following artists who have contributed to this book:

Vanessa Card, Andrew Clark, Chris Forsey, Ron Hayward, Gary Hincks, Richard Hook, John James, Alan Male, Rob McCaig, Terry Riley, Martin Sanders, Guy Smith, Roger Smith, Sue Stitt, Stephen Sweet, Ross Watton, Darrell Warner, Mike White.

The publishers wish to thank the following for supplying photographs for this book:

Page 11 (C/L) British Museum/AKG; 15 (T/L) The British Library/E.T.Archive, (C) The Kobal Collection/E.T.Archive, (C/R) The Victoria and Albert Museum/E.T.Archive, (B) E.T.Archive; 17 (T/R) Dover Publications; 25 (T/L) Gamma/Frank Spooner Pictures; 27 (T) Lah Weston, (C/R) Mark Beesley, (C) Dover Publications; 28 (B/R) Dover Publications; 30 (T) Cherry Williams; 33 (C) Neil Cooper/Panos Pictures.

All other photographs from Miles Kelly archives.